SOUL BATTLE
it's not against flesh and blood

Jill Thompson
December 2006

JILL THOMPSON

Epheseans 6:13
Carlos Rosado

**Evangel
Publishing House**

Nappanee, Indiana 46550

Edited by Kathy Borsa
Cover Design by Matthew Gable

ISBN-10: 1-928915-94-9
ISBN-13: 978-1-928915-94-2
Library of Congress Catalog Control Number: 2006938779

Printed in the United States of America

5 6 7 8 9 EP 8 7 6 5 4 3 2 1

In loving memory of

Jason Rosado

1974-1989

The Spirit of the Sovereign Lord is on me, because the Lord has anointed me to preach good news to the poor. He has sent me to bind up the brokenhearted, to proclaim freedom for the captives and release from darkness for the prisoners,

To proclaim the year of the Lord's favor and the day of vengeance of our God, to comfort all who mourn,

And provide for those who grieve in Zion — to bestow on them a crown of beauty instead of ashes, the oil of gladness instead of mourning, and a garment of praise instead of a spirit of despair.

(Isaiah 61:1-3)

Table of Contents

A word from the editor:

You are in for a fascinating read—the true story of Carlos Rosado and his path to freedom. The author has assigned names to the demons in this story so that the reader can follow them more easily throughout the text. The events are real, but because it is unseen, the portrayal of the spirit world is done through the eyes of the author—based on Carlos' own descriptions.

People are fascinated with the supernatural, but sometimes when it is spoken of as a reality instead of a fantasy, they become skeptical or even frightened. The Word of God has many examples of the enemy's attempts to overcome people, but it also offers the hope of freedom. As in Carlos' story, there are people chained to the powers of darkness because they simply don't know how to break those chains. It is our desire that this story will point you to the truth, and that truth will set you free.

Kathy L. Borsa

Preface

In the winter of 1965, the *New York Herald Tribune* published a series of headline articles entitled "The City in Crisis: New York's Puerto Rican Poverty Trap." Though they could speak and understand no English and had no jobs or lodging awaiting them, these Puerto Ricans—as citizens—were entitled to enter the country at will, which they did by the thousands. It was a time when nearly one-fifth of the city's people lived in poverty conditions—many in cramped, inadequately heated, rat-infested apartments. Middle-class whites, traditionally the heart of the metropolis and its economy, fled to the suburbs to be replaced by 800,000 Puerto Ricans who, for the most part, were unskilled or semi-skilled. More than 70,000 youths roamed the streets, out of work and out of school. And Carlos Rosado was one of those untrained, uncaring youths—until the day he met Jesus Christ.

Soul Battle is the story of how Carlos Rosado survived the killing effects that ghetto life, isolation, and drugs have on the body, the mind, and the spirit. By coming to the saving knowledge of God's love for him through Jesus Christ, Carlos' testimony offers hope and spiritual, battle-winning affirmation not only to the Puerto Rican and Spanish-speaking communities but to teenage audiences as well. Not since *The Cross and the Switchblade* has there been a contemporary book for teens that testifies of God's power and redeeming love in such an authentic way.

The Author

INTRODUCTION

In the beginning was the Word, and the Word was with God, and the Word was God.

(John 1:1)

Balaam was on his way down, sucked into a spin through the tunnel's black void. He writhed and screamed in the agony of terror, desperately clawing at the nothingness around him. He watched the light above him grow distant as he fell deeper into the abyss. With his fall, an eternal plan had been set in motion for all time, and he was on his way to a destiny that he was helpless to change.

Created by God and living in that forever place beyond time, Balaam had been one of the supernatural beings beyond number. They surrounded God's throne as a heavenly council, worshipping and glorifying God continually. Among them, Lucifer, the beautiful angel of light in their midst, had imagined himself greater than God and more worthy of praise. So God had directed His archangel Michael, with the other angels under his authority, to defeat and cast the adversary down to earth along with his followers. And so it was that Lucifer became ruler of the powers of the air, loose in the world with his legions of demons. Among Lucifer's many followers were those like Balaam (the devourer), Azmaveth (strength of death), Baanah (oppression), and Evi (desire).

Balaam's anticipation of the plunge's end was far worse than it actually was. With one great force of momentum, Balaam, Lucifer, and all the demonic agents exploded with exhilarating freedom into earthly existence and spread like wave upon wave of pollution across the waters and lands. Sight unseen, yet spiritually present, the demons occupied the souls and minds of mortals that had prepared a place for them.

In the early days of the fall to earth, Eden, Mesopotamia, and Africa had offered the demons a wealth of opportunity to create illusions of truth. As populations grew and spread across oceans and continents, Lucifer and his angels also spread in popularity, as they were carried along under the guise of traditions and rituals. When the Spaniards and the black slaves imported from Africa arrived in Puerto Rico, the tribal mythology of the Taino people blended with Santerian customs and beliefs. Throughout the Puerto Rican island, enduring tales about demons who roamed after dark pursuing food or people were religiously trusted as truth and passed from generation to generation. For Balaam and the others, this was a hopeful development in Lucifer's grand scheme of things. But there was a down side to it.

Oh, it was true that when they first had arrived in Puerto Rico, Balaam and his kin felt secure in the people's faith in them. But later when they had sought to expand their positions of power, the demons could not deny the one truth that threatened to defeat them even here. It was the truth that God had created mortals in His own image. Unlike the angels or anything else in all of creation, God had created human beings in His likeness, and He loved them—each and every single one. All of the fallen contingent really hated that fact, and it caused them to become increasingly persistent and clever in their strategies to separate the people from that knowledge.

And so the spiritual war that had started in heaven continued on the earth. At times the followers of Lucifer were able to cause men to flee God in guilt or hide in the shadows of despair. Yet because God loved the world so much, He became an inescapable presence in human history, even becoming flesh to live among them for a time. It had been during that time that Balaam had held out a glimmer of hope when it looked for all the world like Lucifer might succeed in his lordship over God's son. Azmaveth had worked particularly hard to live up to his "strength of death" name, along with many others. But when it was finished, God arose victorious and there had been all sorts of demonic casualties in the process. As usual, God had had His angels to bring mortals His word and assistance. He had also given them the life of His Son and later His Spirit. Now people could prevail against the adversary by the sheer power of His name.

Today the war continues to rage on in the souls of the people. The battles are not against flesh but against powers and principalities. If some mortal souls are lost, what does Balaam or any other demon care? Yet there is One who does care, who has always cared. It is He who loves those who are lost, those who are wounded, and those who are prisoners. He has loved them since the beginning—and He knows them by name.

PART ONE

Puerto Rico

Caminante, no hay camino, se hace camino al andar.

(Traveler, there is no path, the path is made as you walk.)

—Antonio Machado (Spanish poet, 1875-1935)

CHAPTER 1

The Spirit of the Sovereign Lord is upon me . . .
(Isaiah 61:1)

With his kite almost airborne, Carlos ran off the edge of the mountain so suddenly that his heart was in his throat before he realized there was no ground beneath him. He was on his way down. In the momentum of the plunge, Carlos heard himself scream out in terror as if the sound could save him.

The breakneck speed with which he catapulted down the ravine caused both breath and panic to explode from the pit of his stomach, yet he remained aware of what was happening to him. Rolling and bouncing, barefoot and shirtless, down through palm brush and banana leaves, an alarming thought rushed through his mind. In this forever fall, it occurred to Carlos that he would probably not stop in time to avoid the river sixty feet below, if he lived that long. And when he hit the river in the end, he'd be too weak to swim or too hurt to pull himself out. *"Voy a morirme!* I'm gonna die!" the boy sobbed as he grabbed desperately at the blurred obstacles spinning by.

He was on his way to death and nothing could prevent it from happening. Nothing that is, except for a well-placed banana tree stump just before the river. Carlos smashed into it with such a solid thud that all thoughts immediately left his seven-year-old mind, and he crumpled down upon the lush, sweet Puerto Rican earth.

It was the birds Carlos heard first, and he imagined them gloriously arrayed in their multitude of colors, curiously twittering back and forth overhead in the palm and mango trees. Any sound that was made on the mountain echoed through the ravines, and every day of his life he had awakened to these sounds. As Carlos opened his eyes, he started to cry. In fact, he lay there for quite a while just crying and crying. It felt good to be able to cry. Carlos cried with pain and relief as he looked back up the slope.

He was amazed to find himself not dead but still alive in paradise. And this land was any boy's paradise. There were banana and fruit trees everywhere. The flowers and animals added such a richness of smells and sounds that Carlos was sure that nowhere else in heaven or on earth could such a glorious place exist. Even his house on the edge of the woods around Mayaguez was simple, yet intricately a part of the tropical countryside. Below him was the river where he and his older brothers Hector and Efrain and his younger brother Izzy spent many hours swimming, messing around, and getting into the kind of trouble that boys turn into legends when they become men.

Carlos cautiously sat up to inspect his dark brown arms and legs. Although Carlos did not yet know it, God had had His hand upon him as he had fallen and missed hitting the most dangerous rocks and trees in the steep ravine. By God's grace, the razor-ridged edges of the palm leaves littering the ground had not slashed the young boy's back to shreds. Carlos' body was unbroken during the fall, but he was still much shaken and covered with more than the usual amount of bruises and scratches.

Bruises and scratches—how often he and his brothers roamed the jungles and rivers with carefree abandon, finding their fun in irresponsible ways with no thought to possible risks. During the rainy seasons, Carlos, his brothers, and cousins all would ride huge banana leaves like runaway sleds, zipping down the muddy riverbanks and slopes. At other times Carlos' mother Anna would send the boys to gather fruit, and days were spent climbing higher and higher into the jungle to find fruit that was fresher and bigger there. The boys would take big sacks up to the Kilometers where the mangos and pineapples grew wild. Following the edge of the mountain up to another river where their swimming holes were, they would take a basket along to catch eel, crabs, and crayfish to bring home. All the while they would play, throw stones, and compete with each other over who would do what on a dare. The boys knew that risky feats were the true measure of a man. That and who was strong enough to carry home the giant rows of bananas on their shoulders.

After a day of adventure, they could not help but return home with injuries. His mother would greet them with "I-told-you-so" and give them a hard time as she tended to their hurts. It seemed to Carlos that anything that required her attention led to a scolding from her. One time Carlos had cut his finger to the bone while peeling an orange. Another time he had cut his hand while slicing a sweet shaft of sugar cane his mouth had been watering for. Each time his mother had applied a bandage but never offered words of sympathy to him. Carlos loved his mother, though he couldn't remember a time when she had embraced him or tousled his hair in that carefree way mothers do when love and affection towards their sons catch them by surprise. Carlos thought perhaps she cared for him, yet protectively hidden away in the boy's heart was the longing to really feel or recognize his mother's love for him.

Carlos and Izzy in Puerto Rico

Now, sitting there in the jungle, he was afraid to go home and explain his condition to his mother. How many times had she told him and his brothers not to go too close to the edge of the mountain? Sure, he had survived the fall, but Carlos had no doubt that his mother would interpret this brush with death as deliberately not listening to her warnings and beat him. It was crazy but Carlos had soon learned to expect her discipline of frustration with him instead of hugs of comfort when he got hurt. Afterwards his mother would say, "*O, ven aquí hijito*, let me fix you up." Even so, he was afraid that his body could not take another assault or scolding after the scare he had just had, and he was hurt so badly this time.

He wiped his eyes with the back of his grimy hand and took a deep, shaky breath. Unsteadily, he pulled himself together and slowly crawled back up the ravine toward home.

The One who loved Carlos, who knew his name, watched as Carlos climbed out of the ravine and went into one of the tin-roofed houses along the dirt path that was the center of their jungle neighborhood. Some distance away, Azmaveth also watched and was annoyed. Though he was sometimes able to amuse himself with death (disguised as accidental occurrences or childish irresponsibility), Azmaveth fiddling with Carlos' kite-flying hadn't amounted to much. However, God's hand on the boy, even at this young age, aroused Azmaveth's curiosity. Perhaps this one would be worth taking captive over the moments of time that make up a human life. Unaware of the spiritual deliberations, Carlos slipped into the kitchen in search of his mother.

CHAPTER 2

Your love is better than life.
(Psalm 63:3)

Anna's lifeless steps slowed as she neared the house. Raising four sons was tiring enough without sewing at the factory each day. Carrying the few groceries she had picked up after work, Anna stepped onto the front stoop and shouldered the door open. It wasn't so much that she hated leaving her children because she missed them as she bent over her sewing machine hour after hour. She just worried some about what happened at home when she left her boys in the care of Virginia, or Petra, or worse—her father Abuelo.

Setting the bag down, Anna went into her room to change out of her work clothes. Slipping her dress over her head, she recalled the time she had come home to find that Abuelo had sold his grandsons to the owner of the coffee mill, and she had needed to go rescue them. Abuelo's abuse of the boys was bad enough, but sold as slave labor? Anna washed her hands and threw water on her face. She cared about her sons, but one mother couldn't do it all! At least she had somebody to watch them while she was working. Anna shook off the mindset of her work day and set about preparing for supper. Her thoughts were well on other things when Carlos slipped into the kitchen.

Carlos was cautiously heartened so see Anna and approached as quietly as his runny nose and stifled sob-breaths would allow. Before she could notice him, Carlos shrugged against the wooden wall, watching, trying to gauge her mood. How beautiful his mother looked to him. Her long, black hair flowed down as a waterfall splashing against bare shoulders and light coffee-cream arms. Her shorts and sleeveless top revealed a neat figure as she moved around the kitchen. After the death of his father, Carlos knew his mother was never at a loss for male companionship. Yet it wasn't just her looks that attracted them. His mother was an industrious woman who confidently took care of her family. Anna worked hard but laughed easily when she would momentarily forget the burden-filled days.

Knowing she would see him eventually, Carlos approached Anna as she turned in his direction. Anna hesitated when she saw Carlos. Thinking he was stopping by the house for something to eat, she started to reach for the rice she was cooking. The boys took care of themselves pretty much for meals, grabbing fruit from the forest in their travels or stopping by the house for rice. Her attention came back to her young son again.

As he stood there in front of her, tear-stained and bruised, Carlos sensed his mother's disapproval and wondered if his battered body was evidence that he had disobeyed her. He couldn't begin to explain. And she, observing his wounds, couldn't begin heaping any more judgment upon him. Anna turned off the rice and took out the galvanized tub to bathe his battered body.

Anna was competent in her Puerto Rican ways that blended together Christian, African, and Caribbean religions and healing practices. Healing came through certain prayers and potions, and Anna knew what leaves and roots to have her sons gather to squeeze out the juice and burn it at her shrines if needed. One time Carlos had eaten too many shrimp and boils had erupted all over his body. Anna had heated some milk with raisins in it and gave it to Carlos to drink. The boils had gone away.

Silently washing the cuts on his arms, she noticed his hands; they were Neri's hands. It surprised her and she glanced up at Carlos' face. He had his father's hazel green eyes and dark complexion too. She left Carlos to rest awhile, sighing and pondering as she put things away.

Anna had married Neri despite the objections of her parents. While Neri was not a black man—for her father harbored a deep prejudice toward Africans—Neri was dark-skinned enough to create resentment. Still, their life together had started out fine. Anna had worked in the fields bundling up and tossing onto wagons the stalks of sugar cane that Neri and the other men cut down with their machetes. At least they had jobs and easy glimpses of good times flashed when Anna had first loved Neri. He was manly and sociable, and his own brand of love provided her with food money before he gambled.

Love—it was Carlos and the oldest son Hector that Neri truly loved. Shrouded in the mists of Anna's memory, she saw Neri approach the house, after a late night of gambling all his money away, calling to his boys. With uncontained joy, Hector and Carlos darted out toward their slightly drunk but affectionate hero. As a toddler, Carlos' uncanny resemblance to Neri was unmistakable. Neri swung Carlos up unto his shoulders and, with a hand resting on Hector's head, steered the boys out of the darkness into the light where Anna waited. Slapping her around would come later.

Anna closed her eyes, hand on the counter's wooden edge, fighting her emotions as the intensely real memories of Neri washed over her. His brand of love also included the smoky-rum camaraderie of the cock fights and his reputation of excellence as a fighter, one who controlled both life and wife with an educated fist. Instead of nostalgic longing for a dead husband, difficult remembrances of Neri rekindled anger within Anna. Even now, when she thought of his death, she started to seethe.

As usual after work, Neri had found his way to one of the liquor storefronts that perched along the weed-cracked walkways of the town. Evi had whispered to the men throughout the dry, hot day, and evening's release and the desire to quench their thirst with bottled spirits was strong in their minds. Masculine voices and the odors of sweat-dampened cotton, work clothes mingled together in the fading light as each went in to buy their rum, then rejoined their friends loitering outside.

This evening Azmaveth circled among the men as well. He blew into the swigs and murmurings of their emptying bottles, and he breathed on the machetes most of them carried. Neri and his friends knew each other well. They laughed and argued together until they were drunk enough to face what was waiting for them at home with dominance and enjoyment. As Neri turned to go, voices rose and shoving began so abruptly that it took awhile for the men to recognize a fight. One man's arm was slashed, and then a vengeful swing of a machete sliced into Neri, almost completely severing his head. He crumpled to the ground, dead.

Across the way the young boy who delivered Anna's groceries watched in unbelief as the men shuffled around Neri's body debating what to do. The boy heard their talk of hiding the murder from Anna, for they thought with four little ones, the woman might go into shock or hysterics. Staggering slightly, the men lifted Neri's body, careful to hold on his head, and weaved off to the house of Anna's brother. The wide-eyed boy shot off to Anna's house. The show over, a satisfied Azmaveth sailed off to find Evi.

"What do you think I am, a girl? A baby? I'm no girl and no baby! I'm a grown woman, I can take this," Anna had shouted at them when they finally brought Neri's boxed and bloody body to her. After hearing the news from the grocery boy, Anna had time to grow enraged at the thought of the men carrying Neri from place to place instead of bringing him home for her to tend to. Over the next couple of days, she mourned and cried but Neri was not a good man, and it was hard to cry for long.

Deep in the heavenly Father's heart was the eternal longing to reach Anna with the truth that the darkness that drives murder of the flesh is the same spirit that steals the soul. There were demonic spirits about, but for Anna and the folks of the town like her, the fear, the screams, and yells in the night were part of the culture they lived in. How to deal with spiritual powers had been passed down to her from generations back, and that was all she knew. Yet as it was, God's love would always be to her a dim shadow, patiently present and waiting until a time when she would be able to see Him clearly.

Meanwhile, she would continue to care for her sons the only ways she knew how—and to pray faithfully to the shrines in her room. Knowing she did this, Carlos had come to depend on his mother to have his best interest at heart. He was fascinated with her statue of a warrior angel with wings. It had dark brown skin, a sword in its hand, and was stepping on a dragon. Anna had saints too—big figures of saints. Carlos knew they were carefully arranged, the biggest ones in the middle. She had hung a rosary from the neck of one of them. Carlos had seen her burn incense and other things in a little brown base that looked like cement but was made out of wood. Carlos didn't know what she was praying for then but, with Neri dead, Anna had sought provision and a false sense of safety by any power she knew that was part of the spiritual world. While Carlos and his brothers thought of her as a religious lady—none of them knew what she was really bowing down to.

CHAPTER 3

He will quiet you with his love.
(Zephaniah 3:17)

Carlos' life in the mountains included simple joys and grand adventures that would remain in his heart all his life. It stayed light until 8:30 or 9:00 at night. The hills of coffee beans all around were beautiful in his sight as they changed over seasons from green to yellow to red. Going to town once a month for rice, flour, or beans was a half-day's walk down the mountain, but it was worth it to see the cars.

June to November was the rainy season and the steady storms would flood everything. Carlos was grateful to be living up the mountain above the river. The rain on their tin roof often sounded as if coconuts were falling down on their house. It didn't take long for the river to overflow and form a current so swift that debris and dead animals were caught up in it. At the sight of dead cows or horses floating by, Carlos would feel slightly sorry about having thrown stones at them in teasing.

During the summer it was paradise to walk around without a shirt or shoes and not bothered by humidity. On their way to play in the forest, the boys would take sticks along because they all hated snakes. One good hit would knock them out of the way.

This day Carlos was first to wake up. Though his body felt like stretching, it was difficult to do while he was still in bed. Hector, Efrain, and Izzy all shared the one bed with Carlos in their little bedroom off the kitchen. While it was nice to have company at night, now the morning sun and his brothers' bodies were making him too warm and he was starting to get squirmy. Anxious to start the day, Carlos got up and headed to the outdoor latrine.

"Hey, Litito! Tony!" He could hear Efrain yelling at the house across from theirs on the little dirt road that ran through the neighborhood. Carlos jumped off the front porch and skidded to a halt beside Hector and Efrain at the edge of the road.

"Junior!" Carlos yelled almost as loud as his big brother. Junior, Litito, and Tony were some of their cousins, and Junior, like Carlos, was about three years younger than the rest.

"Cut it out, Carlos. I already called 'em."

"Hey, Juuuunior!" Carlos yelled even louder.

"Why you . . ." Efrain reached for the scruff of Carlos' neck.

"Hey, Efrain!" Litito's shout back interrupted. "Man, it's too hot to walk on the dirt. Get some leaves and come on over."

Carlos and his brothers didn't have to search long to find banana leaves suitable for shoes. They tied the leaves onto their bare feet and walked gingerly across the road. At 115 degrees, the finely packed dirt had heated up beyond scorching, and the soles of their feet, though toughened, wouldn't have withstood even the hop, skip, and jump distance that separated their houses. After the brothers and cousins got together, they hurried off through the tropical forest on their way to the coffee mill. "They haven't come by for the shipment yet," Tony was saying.

"Alright, let's head over there and see how it's going," Hector replied as he held aside lower branches so that Carlos, Junior, and Izzy could troop along without getting smacked in the face.

Carlos and the other little guys were always trying to compete and keep up with the older boys. It came naturally to them to see who could climb up the coconut trees the fastest and cut the coconuts down with machetes. It was always about who could do things the fastest, who could swim the furthest, who could dive the deepest. Carlos, Junior, and Izzy were often along when Hector, Efrain, and the others, would go up as high as they could in the Kilometers, where the diving was good and they didn't have to worry about hitting any rocks on the way down. Sometimes they'd go up as much as thirty or forty feet and then dive. Carlos' gaze would follow the falling bodies from the top to the plunge and desire more than anything in the world to be a part of this bond the older boys shared. He would leap off at ten or fifteen feet just to make a point, but he was too scared to go much higher than that. Carlos admired his brothers' confidence and fearlessness in the face of danger, and he longed to be like them.

The coffee mill was not far from town and they got there in record time. All around the plant were mounds and mounds of coffee beans just sitting there waiting for a bunch of boys to have a good time in.

"Ahhhhhhyaaa!" Plumpfff. They all jumped in. They had a great time rolling down the fragrant mounds of coffee beans. This mound, then that one, fell victim to their king-of-the-hill antics. Carlos picked up a handful and threw it up into the air. Flicking beans off his shoulder, Junior tossed a handful back at Carlos. Soon they were all throwing beans at each other.

"Hey, you kids, get away from there!" Coming into view and stalking very quickly towards them was the owner. "Get off of there!" he threatened and bent over to pick up a stick to throw at them.

"Whoa, we're outta here!" Efrain said stopping only for a split second where they were poised in action on the bean hills. The next minute there were kids scrambling everywhere to beat it to the tree line. Uh-oh, the owner was picking up stones and stuff to throw.

"Hey, you kids!" But those kids were not anything if not fast. Safely undercover they broke into fits of laughter and reveled in the "Did-you-sees . . ." It had definitely been worth the risk of getting caught or, worse yet, somebody telling their parents what they had been doing. It always amazed them how their mother found out about the trouble they had gotten into during the day. But that was one of the disadvantages of a close-knit community.

Carlos depended on the things that were predictable in his life. He depended on his sense of total belonging to this tropical land. He knew his place among the brothers and cousins, which gave his life purpose. It was all he wanted.

The boys wandered away from the coffee mill and spent the rest of the day messing around near one of their swimming holes. Lying on his stomach next to Izzy after climbing out of the muddy water, Carlos watched the small ground creatures crawling by.

"Look," said Izzy, "I bet I can hit that bug from here with this stick."

"Go ahead and try," Carlos dared him.

The stick landed too far and the bug, bumping into the stick in its path, deftly climbed over it and continued on its way.

"Ha!" Carlos smirked.

"Stupid bug," Izzy growled and ground the bug into the dirt with his bare hand.

Carlos rolled over on his back. Gazing at the green canopy above them, he could see shimmering patches of sky and brightly colored birds in the treetops. "Hey, Izzy. See that leaf up there on the second branch? I bet I can hit it with this stick." Izzy rolled on his back to watch. Carlos missed.

"Ha-ha yourself, Carlos!"

"Aw, a stick has too much drag." Carlos stood up to look for a stone. Izzy was following him when Junior came loping along beside them.

"Hey, want to see me hit the water with this rock all the way from here?" asked Junior finding a hefty stone. He heaved it up into the air. The splash signaled success.

Escalating into a competition, sticks and stones and coconuts were soon flying everywhere. Aiming up high into a tree, Carlos threw a rock at a hanging mango. Missed. He scooped up a handful of stones and whipped them as hard as he could up into the branches. Some of them showered back down upon him and he had to cover his head. One last rock. A bird landed on the branch above the mango fruit. Carlos sent the rock flying, missed the mango, and hit the little bird. Its beautiful, perfect body plummeted down and landed dead at Carlos' feet.

The boys gathered around him. Carlos looked up and met Hector's gentle eyes. Efrain and Izzy started jumping up and down yelling, "Way to go, Carlos, you got it, you got it!" Standing there over the dead bird, something twisted so hard inside of Carlos that he wanted to throw up. He had had no intention of killing the bird. In that moment Carlos realized that the ultimate prize of his thoughtless game had been a life taken, and he wished he could take the rock back. He also discovered that his tender heart could not handle the death of an innocent creature. The bird had done nothing but be there. Later, when they went home, his mother found out from the brothers that Carlos had killed a bird.

Angry at him and wanting to be sure he wouldn't kill any more birds, she told him, "Listen, Carlos. You shouldn't have killed that bird today because now, when you die, that bird is going to come and pluck your eyes out."

Then the night had come. The brothers in the bed went quickly to sleep, but sleep was no longer an escape for Carlos. With sleep came the nightmare reality about what his mother had told him would happen. He dreamed he was dead and was running from the bird through the forest, through the palm trees, through the sugar cane. Running and shaking with terror. In his haste to get away, Carlos would trip and fall. Looking back, he saw the bird swooping down at him, coming right down to savagely peck at his flesh and pluck out his eyes—his own hazel green eyes.

CHAPTER 4

From the lips of children and infants you have ordained praise because of your enemies, to silence the foe and the avenger.
(Psalm 8:2)

Carlos' grandfather visited the family often. With Neri gone from his daughter's life, Abuelo felt secure in his authoritative meddling. His beautiful daughter marrying that dark-skinned Neri simmered such a wrath in Abuelo that it consumed his soul and played out in the satisfied sport he found in tormenting Neri's sons. The spirit of Banaah (oppression) found comfort within Abuelo, and his role as dutiful patriarch only thinly disguised the meanness of his spirit.

"Carlos, Izzy, did you know that I can blow smoke out of my eyes?" Abuelo called to them. Abuelo was leisurely smoking one of his big, fat cigars. He took another long, slow drag as the boys watched. Carlos had thought that it was quite impossible for smoke to really come out of someone's eyeballs but he wasn't sure. His grandfather spoke with such confidence that if such a thing could be done, he believed Abuelo could surely do it.

"Come closer and see if you can see the smoke coming out of my eyes," Abuelo said as he eased down on the porch steps more to their level. Carlos and Izzy looked at each other, so tempted by the possibility. They hesitantly inched forward. Abuelo took a dramatic puff on the cigar perched between his wrinkled brown fingers. Carlos smelled the familiar scent of Abuelo's cigar-smoke.

"Closer, now watch my eyes. Closer . . ." Abuelo encouraged. His lips and breath played with the smoke shapes escaping his mouth and Carlos and Izzy were mesmerized as they leaned in toward him. Carlos looked deep into his grandfather's eyes.

He had looked upon Abuelo's face all his young life and he knew every inch of it. Carlos could see the weathered skin of his cheeks, the lines on his forehead, and the dark, dark color of his eyes. Even though familiar, there was still something uncomfortable and hidden about Abuelo that Carlos could not quite trust. But here was his grandfather, his own flesh and blood kin. And even though Carlos' mind reasoned that a grandfather would never deceive his own grandson, his heart always weakened when he gazed into the blackness of Abuelo's eyes. Yet, Carlos was intrigued and searched for the smoke.

With Carlos and Izzy intently locking eyes with Abuelo, and his own return gaze never wavering, Abuelo slowly lowered his unseen cigar hand and abruptly stabbed their arms and legs with the smoldering stogie. Abuelo burst into laughter at their shrieks of confusion and pain, thoroughly enjoying the surprise of burning them with his cigar.

Later, as Abuelo was calmly savoring the last of his cigar, he thought to himself how gullible the boys were. Smoke out the eyes—ha! Why he could get them to believe anything he could dream up. He took another puff and stared thoughtfully at the cigar he rolled between his thumb and forefinger. It was a bad thing, though, how weak and easy those boys were to fool. And another thing was that they often went their own way and didn't obey their mother well enough. Carlos and his brothers needed a real man to raise them up right, keen-minded and respectful. It was a good thing he was around, Abuelo thought. He blew the last ring of smoke up into the air and went off to find rocks to throw at the river rats straggling by the back porch.

Carlos had needed to get away from his grandfather—fast. Disappearing into the forest alone, he sought the safety and comfort of the outdoors. A short distance from home, he sat down under a tree, hugged his knees to his chest, and put his head down, still sniffling and smarting from the burns on his leg. He didn't want to venture too far in the woods alone. In thinking things over, Carlos valiantly struggled to understand the adults in his life. In the end, though, he gave up on what he could not comprehend. At least he would always be able to survive the hurts as long as he could escape into the tropical paradise around him. Carlos leaned his head back against the tree trunk and let out a deep sigh. His eyes moved up towards the sky as he listened to himself breathe. Breathe in . . . the pure, sweet Puerto Rican air filling his lungs and his spirit. Breathe out . . . exhaling the frets and fears. His heart calmed, Carlos felt profound peace in the beautiful world around him.

Sometimes when Carlos considered the heavens above him and the creatures and land all around, he felt very small and defenseless, not able to control anything about his life because it was the adults who were in charge of him. Carlos didn't know how much God loved him in those moments of hurt, and why it was that being in the midst of God's creation brought peace within his soul. Carlos had run right into God's arms when he had run into the woods and surrendered all the circumstances that were beyond a child's understanding. And he found favor in God's sight, for surely the boy had praised God just by reveling in the works of His hand.

Abuelo did indeed continue with what he sensed as his disciplinary role in the family. Carlos' grandfather did more correcting than ever when he would overhear Anna scolding her sons. "You should give those boys a whipping," Abuelo would shout. "It's what they deserve. Here, I'll teach them a lesson they won't soon forget!" And he was as brutal with his thick heavy belt as he was with his pleasure in using it.

Because Abuelo not only indulged himself in cigars but also rum, his frequent drink would make him feel powerful, and he'd punish the boys for whatever reason he could think of. Sometimes he would beat them just because he had forgotten to do it for a while. Though Anna would sometimes holler at Abuelo about it, there were not too many times that she got in front of him to defend her children.

Theirs was a small house, and when Abuelo was after them, there weren't a lot of places Carlos could run. Sometimes the boys would jump under their bed to get away, but Abuelo would get down and pull them out. With no place to hide, the boys would run outside to find refuge. But no matter, Abuelo was patient with punishment, knowing the boys would be home at dark. He knew they were terrified of the dark. Abuelo would just make himself comfortable on the front porch and wait to beat them when they got home. And Abuelo never, ever forgot what he was waiting for.

CHAPTER 5

I will fear no evil, for you are with me.
(Psalm 23:4)

As the spirit world of Banaah, Evi, and Balaam gathered strength in the evening, fear of what evil might be in the forest would indeed drive the boys home. Abuelo was not wrong about that. The familiar joys of the day transformed into foreboding when menacing shadows gathered and the light faded from every lane and leaf of their neighborhood. Deep in the trees Carlos had seen Evi (desire) beckoning to him, suggestive eyes and motioning hands calling for him to come into the woods. Too young to understand why he trembled at the temptation, it was the fear of never being able to come back that made Carlos avert his eyes and keep walking. He was aware of the spiritual presences for day's end was a time of darkness in more ways than one.

Anna saw in Carlos a sensitivity to matters of heart and spirit, which made him so different from her other sons. He, like her, could feel the oppression when daylight faded. When he would sometimes be startled awake by shrieks and screams of agony outside in the night, Anna never explained them to Carlos, nor did she want to because she thought it would scare him. But it hadn't made any difference. Even without explanation or ever having seen any horror stories on TV or heard them on the radio (since they did not own either), Carlos knew something out there could get him if given opportunity.

Carlos' brothers, though not in tune with the unseen, were also afraid of "out there." If they had to go to the bathroom during the night, fear would keep them in bed. Carefully holding it in like water balloons filled to bursting, they finally could stand it no longer and would seek relief at the outdoor latrine in pairs. Leaving the bed at night was frightening. And so it was that when night came, Carlos and his brothers did not venture outside, and once they were in bed, they did not want to leave it.

As nighttime happenings swirled on around him, Carlos' sleep was visited by glimpses of evil that intruded without warning. Sometimes in his shallow rest, dead birds were lying in wait and he'd wake up crying in terror when the pain of beak on flesh was too terrific to bear. In his desperation, Carlos did everything he could possibly do to sleep dreamlessly throughout the night. During the day he played hard and stretched the limits of his physical endurance so that exhaustion rendered him oblivious to sounds in the night, the darkness, and the need to go to the outhouse. But sometimes it didn't work.

Settling down in their bed together one night, the brothers had one by one started to drift off into the saving world of deep sleep. Carlos peered around the room at the shadows trailing down the walls. Out of the corner of his eye, he saw movement. Turning, his head cradled in his elbow, Carlos squinted hard along the edges of the ceiling. It was not easy to see depth in the darkness—to tell what was real or illusion. He heard the bed creak and Carlos made out the silhouette of Hector's back as he shifted his weight to the other side. Carlos closed his eyes conjuring up a happy picture of the forest during the day. He was out among the flowering trees poised for play.

As he was about to escape into his dream paradise, something poked his shoulder. Carlos opened his eyes. Lying there a minute, he waited to see if it happened again. He felt a tug at his hair. Carlos rolled onto his back and looked across the bodies in the bed. Efrain's head came up. A few shoves were exchanged between him and Hector.

The bed shook slightly and Carlos lay back down. He listened to Izzy breathing next to him and could tell he was awake. Carlos felt a tug at his hair again, only this time the urgent pull was coming from under the bed. Izzy must have felt it too since he jerked upright and grabbed onto Carlos. "Leave me alone . . . *stop* it!" The brothers soon realized that what they weren't doing to each other was being done by something under the bed and surrounding them in their room. All four were being drawn under by pulls and tugs and Carlos could feel his body start to slide over the edge, to be swallowed into the darkness. They held onto each other to keep from being pulled under, clinging and screaming.

Anna came to the doorway. Alarmed to realize the boys weren't just goofing around, she rushed into the midst of the commotion, desperate to save her sons from the spirits that filled the room. Uttering words that he could not understand, Carlos watched his mother grab at the air and throw demons out the open window. He couldn't believe his eyes as he watched his mother battle the unseen enemy.

The next day Carlos asked his mother what had happened in the night. "Don't worry about it," Anna had replied. "You were dreaming. I never came into your room."

"But, something was pulling me under. Something was there!"

"You were dreaming, Carlos. Just forget about it. Don't even think about those kinds of things."

The surreal events of the night were unforgettable, and Carlos needed to know the truth about what had happened. But they never spoke of it again nor did he discuss it with his brothers. Carlos was left to conjure up his worst fears alone, and still, he wondered what to make of it. For the next several nights, Anna burned coals and put them in a pot. Sweeping it around their room, she would spread smoke like a blanket of protection all over and under the bed.

Carlos could now see stuff coming into their house at night and he would wake up screaming. His brothers would tell him to be quiet, that he was waking everybody up. Hector would reach over and shake him. "Wake up! You're screaming again." His dead bird nightmares turned into being dragged under the bed, being slashed with nails, or with sharp claws, and his sleep became haunted. Whenever he tried to share his dreams with his mother, she'd tell him not to worry about it. Carlos tried desperately not to worry about it, not to believe that the spirit world was real. Still, there were the shadows by the door, and in his dreams that single bird was waiting for him in the treetops.

CHAPTER 6

*Let the little children come to me . . . for
the kingdom of God belongs to such as
these.*
(Luke 18:15)

Carlos was busy lining up rocks along the weathered railing
of the back porch. He and Izzy had collected quite a few that
morning so they'd be ready when rats came by from the river. It
also kept them from straying too far today. That old Virginia
might need them for something. Carlos' fingers traced the gran-
ite ribbon that divided the smooth brown stone in his hand. His
life in Puerto Rico was never without his mother or without
Virginia.

He figured Virginia was related in some way, but Carlos had
yet to discover the relationships of the adults in his life. He just
knew that she lived across the street. She seemed old to Carlos, her
face like crumpled-up, dark brown paper, smoothed out again
under a thick mane of stark white hair. She was small in stature, but
there was something big in the kind of power that Virginia had. He
thought perhaps she was a witch, and Carlos and his brothers were
afraid of her. When Virginia told them to do something, they did it
in a hurry rather than risk God's punishment on them. She might
even ask Carlos to do something right now, since she had come
across the street to help deliver the new baby.

Brown stones, gray stones, just the right size stones, marched
along the railing like the people that came and went so easily.
Once a man called Estevan had been around the house for a short
time but then he was gone. Now another person, a baby, was
coming into his world but that would be okay eventually. Carlos

knew that babies were women's work, and he vaguely remembered Izzy as a baby. But now Izzy was part of the barefoot gang that roamed each mild-weathered day in their paradise. Another little brother would add playing strength to their numbers when he got old enough. Yes, Carlos would be glad for another brother.

Late in the day Maria was born. And the rats never came by. Izzy ended up throwing the stones at birds and Carlos concluded that nothing was ever really for sure.

It was time for another fiesta. A holiday celebration or a New Year's party, it didn't matter, the boys loved any fiesta for two big reasons. The food was plentiful and the grown-ups' attention was diverted from them for a while. The aroma of pateles and panadias jumbled together with excited conversation, and laughter gave the house a life of its own. Chairs had appeared and were placed according to the proximity of the rum and the record player but allowing room to mingle. The adults would be drinking and dancing to music that spoke wonderful rhythms to Carlos and drew his whole body into song. Everything was made ready and soon the people came. There were friends and relatives, Carlos' cousins, even Virginia's brother Johnny, all came looking for a good time.

Carlos and Junior hung together, watching the grown-ups and laughing, as the party grew louder and more reckless. The boys entertained themselves by eating pateles till they supposed that they had outeaten any man. They wandered around the party helping themselves to fun and whatever the adults' distraction would allow. They could have gotten away with secret swigs of rum if they were interested but, instead, they carefully stole one of Abuelo's cigars. With winks and nudges back and forth, Carlos and Junior slipped outside, smuggling a pack of matches and the cigar between them.

The house was built upon stilts of modest height. That way when the rains came, the flood waters remained below. The level of the house also discouraged animals from coming in, although without screens or shutters on the open windows, chickens and birds were apt to find their way inside anyway to find forgotten food or to satisfy bird-brained curiosity. Because of the stilts, too, a kid could hide nicely underneath if they were small enough, or below a window ledge, which came in handy just now. Junior and Carlos pressed into an unnoticed niche just beneath the back sill.

"Where is it...where is it?" Junior spoke in nervous whispers.

Carlos pulled out the cigar from under his shirt. It was like a part of Abuelo was there with them. The dangerous part.

"Can you get it?" Carlos watched Junior fumble with the matches. Finally the match flamed and Carlos held out the end of the cigar for Junior to light.

"I bet I can blow smoke out of my eyes," Carlos told Junior. The anticipation of Junior's amazement when he mastered the trick made the cigar shake.

"Come on, Carlos. Hold it."

The match fizzled out. Junior lit another. Huddled there by the window, Carlos again held out the cigar towards the small flame. How do you light these things anyway? Could it be this hard? The flame licked the end of the cigar but by the time the match burned out, there still wasn't a smoldering tip to be seen. Carlos put the cigar in his mouth and tried to puff. Nothing.

"Try again," he held the cigar out to Junior, spitting a tobacco crumb off his tongue. Junior lit the match with more confidence now. He held it to the cigar Carlos stretched out unwavering. Through the window above them, they heard someone enter the bedroom. The match went out. They hesitated, looking up at the window and then looked at each other. Carlos gave Junior a try again kind of sigh, and Junior, shrugging, took out another match.

As they hunkered down there, voices drifted out the open window. Carlos, still holding the cigar, recognized his mother's voice. He couldn't quite make out what she was saying. At the sound of her laughter mingled with a man's rumbled tones, Carlos squeezed Junior's arm signaling silence. Edging closer to the window, Carlos slowly unfolded himself to come level with the sill, his eyes just barely above the frame. He felt Junior's body pressed against his as they tried to peer into the room.

It was Johnny that was with Anna in the room, their arms around each other. They weren't laughing just now as their embrace had turned to kisses. Johnny buried his face in her hair and whispered, "We've got to get away from here . . . to start a new life together."

Anna leaned away from him to look into his eyes. "Wha—what are you saying?" her smile turned incredulous.

"America, Anna. Let's go to America!"

"But..."

"Everything is there, Anna!" Johnny released her body but still had her hands clasped in his as he drew her into the idea.

"We can get jobs, good jobs. There's opportunity there, Anna, to make money—so much money. Here we'll always be poor and struggling. In America we can be as rich as we want!"

Carlos sank down again by the window, holding the unlit cigar and thinking how awful it would be to really leave this place. Junior eventually settled down next to him, and together they listened as Johnny pleaded, and soon convinced Anna, that true happiness and wealth waited for them in America. As they made plans, Carlos didn't want to believe that anybody in their right mind could leave this paradise for anyplace else. But Carlos' beliefs, just like predicting when rats would appear or who would be born, didn't make for sure the things he took for granted.

PART TWO

New York City

"Though they could speak and understand no English, though they had only $23.65 left in their pockets, and though they had no jobs or lodging awaiting them, they—as citizens—were entitled to enter the country at will."

—Barry Gottehrer and Claude Lewis
The Herald Tribune (Monday, February 1, 1965)

CHAPTER 7

Even to your old age and gray hairs I am
he, I am he who will sustain you. I have
made you and I will carry you; I will
sustain you and I will rescue you.
(Isaiah 46:4)

The lights of the city were beginning to flicker on as the drunks and the working girls found their positions among the steamy grates and the devil-may-care taxis that dotted New York's Third Avenue. The pretzel vendors of the day had closed up their carts and coals to wheel off into the fading dusk. A few last businessmen, clutching their briefcases and *Herald Tribunes*, were straggling toward the trains that would shuttle them home across the Hudson to the suburbs of New Jersey. The city stood poised for the next round.

Framing this January setting were the outlines of metal garbage cans guarding the curb, mangled and dusted with dingy snow. Reeking and stuffed with rejected Christmas ornaments, one can was nearly knocked over by a mufflerless, green Chevy that staggered to a stop nearby. The car doors opened and adults, kids, luggage, and a jumble of Spanish voices spilled out en masse into the cold streets and shiny sidewalks.

Harsh air and stark surroundings assaulted eleven-year-old Carlos as soon as he climbed out of the borrowed car. However interesting the trip had been (for the foreign sights and smells were everywhere) he was ready to be done with it all. His eyes and heart ached for the lushness of forest green and the chatter of birds. The lushes Carlos saw here took human form, and the bird voices were replaced by the continual hum of traffic. He shivered inside the thin, cotton jacket someone had given him before leaving Puerto Rico. The icy wind cut into his bare legs. He followed his mother and brothers up dirty steps into the apartment building. Johnny, the one who had started all this, was not with them.

It had been only hours ago that they left the island amidst embraces and tears. Carlos and his brothers had bravely started out to the waiting plane, but up close the immenseness of the four-propeller plane had stopped them short. The cabin air smelled different, and the cramped space and noise did nothing to ease the nervousness Carlos felt as a first-time flyer. The centrifugal force of take-off, then the unanticipated air pockets, bounced them until their brains rattled and flip-flopped their stomachs up into their throats. Gripping the airsick bag close, Carlos found himself repeating "*Voy a morirme,* I'm gonna die," like a chant over and over in his head as he puked his way through the sky. He never marveled at the sparkling ocean below, nor did he see the glorious rays of sunlight piercing the fluffy cloud-mountains as if heavenly places were just beyond.

Approaching Idlewild Airport, Carlos had finally pressed a clammy forehead to the cold glass of the tiny window to see what lay before them. The city looked like a miniature building set that had been set directly upon water. Carlos looked across the expanse to see a long, dark strip surrounded by whiteness. The plane banked left and descended making his ears pop, and he was nauseated all over again. But before he could find the little blue bag, the wheels touched the runway, and Carlos was pressed forward then back again into the seat he shared with Izzy. He felt a reassuring squeeze on his arm. It was Hector. They were finally down, but nothing was over—in fact, it was just beginning.

The plane doors opened and a freezing breeze rushed around them. Carlos had never felt anything like it in his life. Way off in the distance, he could see the terminal building. Hesitantly, carrying their meager possessions, they stepped out into the cold and the snow for the long walk.

Snow. Carlos had never heard the word before and now here was this amazing stuff lying all around them. Snow. The boys bent down and touched it. It was cold and crystally clean and white. Carlos put some in his mouth. It tasted so good. Efrain and Izzy were fairly dancing about it when Carlos noticed steam coming from their noses.

"Look what happens when I breathe!" Efrain blew into the air and a brief cloud appeared. Whoa, this is amazing, Carlos thought. They were smoking now. And they smoked and they shivered and they ate snow until finally they reached the terminal.

After hooking up with relatives and piling into the waiting car, Carlos became thoughtful as he rode along looking out the window. Perhaps coming to a place such as this had been a crazy dream, for who could have imagined snow and breath you could see. Perhaps the plan to live here in this noisy, concrete jungle would be acknowledged as a mistake—after all, Johnny wasn't here to convince his mother that she had to stay. Perhaps in a few days Carlos would wake up to the sounds of Puerto Rico again, and he could take off these stupid shoes that hurt his feet and run barefoot in the warmth of his own island; perhaps . . .

*Izzy, Hector, Carlos, and Maria just before
leaving Puerto Rico*

CHAPTER 8

Those who were my enemies without cause hunted me like a bird. They tried to end my life in a pit . . . I thought I was about to be cut off.
(Lamentations 3:52-54)

Tio Hernando had a two-bedroom apartment in the poor, Puerto Rican section of New York City. When Carlos' mother (who was Tio Hernando's sister) had decided to come to America with her children, Hernando had offered them a place to stay, though it was the worst kind of place to move a family into. Anna was just grateful to have a destination at least, but Carlos questioned his mother's soundness of mind after coming through the door of the apartment that first night.

Anna and Maria were given one of the small bedrooms that opened onto the cramped hallway leading off the living room. A tiny bathroom was wedged between that bedroom and a second bedroom occupied by Tio Hernando. A kitchen opened off the other side of the living room. In the kitchen a buzzing, fluorescent bulb cast shadows on the metal cupboards that once-upon-a-time had been white. A pink and gray Formica table was pushed against the large, rather gritty window that had an ancient fire escape, like prison bars, crowding the view. As they gathered in the living room to make sleeping arrangements, Carlos kept an eye on the old, overheating radiator as it clanked and sizzled.

Izzy leaned against Carlos. "I gotta go," he whispered.

"Yeah, me too," Carlos answered listening to the watery sounds steaming from the radiator.

They interrupted the grown-ups in mid-conversation with their need of facilities, and Tio Hernando said, "There, go in that room. And there's a seat there." Izzy followed Carlos into the bathroom. The boys looked for a seat or a chair or something to sit on as Tio Hernando had directed. They looked at the commode and tried to figure it out. Carlos lifted the lid, then flipped the other horseshoe shaped lid up and thought, "Is this—a seat?" Izzy tried it, sitting on the cold porcelain that was too slick and too big. He slipped into the water with a sudden splash. "This is not good," said Carlos and they pondered again how to use this thing. Izzy watched as Carlos carefully placed his left foot on the rounded edge and hauled himself up. Holding onto the walls for balance, he placed his right foot on the other side and stood up. This must be how you use this thing. When Carlos was done, he helped Izzy to stand up on the edge and hold the wall. Finished, they went back to find out more about this crazy place.

Carlos, watching everything and saying nothing, pressed close to Hector. Carlos was surprised to see that Tio Hernando was crippled, and he couldn't help but stare at him in disbelief. Even though Tio Hernando managed to get around the apartment in his wheelchair, his limitations made it difficult for him to keep his place very clean. All Carlos knew for sure was that the place was loud and it smelled bad. A record player blared down the stairwell, and somewhere he could hear a couple swearing at each other. There were roaches and bugs and cars and sirens. No peace, no quiet, no crickets in the night.

That first night they pushed several chairs together so the boys could sleep on them. Some were in the living room, but Carlos had ended up sleeping on two peeling vinyl chairs in the kitchen. Falling into an exhausted sleep, Carlos dreamed he was running through the sugar cane, savoring the heat of the sun on his upturned face. As he paused a moment, an awful foreboding came upon him. Turning, he saw a hideous old woman looking straight at him, her eyes flaming as if to consume his own eyes with her gaze. Carlos cried out as he watched the woman release birds with huge claws and flesh-tearing beaks to swoop with savage strength right for him. He ran as fast as he could through the fields until he found himself among hills and hills of coffee beans stretching out forever. He could feel the hot air from the pursuing birds, expecting to feel the dagger of claws on his back at any moment. He was running and running but kept slipping on the beans as they made a mighty rushing sound of bean against bean sifting under his feet. The rushing sound got louder and louder until Carlos bolted up from his sleep with a panicked gasp. Heart pounding, he realized a train was rushing by on tracks so close to the apartment that the sound had invaded his very presence of mind. He lay back on the chairs, breathing and listening to the trains that would run throughout the night. "One of these days, we're going back because I know my mom hates it here," he thought. "I cannot wait to go back to Puerto Rico."

Besides being noisy and smelly, Carlos discovered that this place was dangerous as well. But it was a different danger than he had ever known. In Puerto Rico, the dangerous risks could be first considered, then chosen, like picking out the most luscious fruit or selecting what kind of physical feats would bring the most honor. At home, danger was attractive because getting past it without harm brought a thrill of freedom and proof of inner strength. Dive the highest, climb the farthest, swim the fastest. Here, though, danger was in their ears, in their eyes, and lying in wait for them on the sidewalks and streets. Here there was no choice. They were forced to face the dare of danger every single time they walked out of the apartment. Pretty soon their freedom was overrun by bullies who were fighting poverty and the ugliness of desperate circumstances in which most of the neighborhood folks found themselves. Carlos' esteem and inner strength that had started to emerge in paradise withered away, for now his young life was entirely about survival.

As time passed Carlos tried to get used to the drunks that were lying around most of the time. They would reach out shaky hands to grab at his clothes when he and his brothers gingerly edged their way past them. With mustered strength and hopeful whines, they begged and pleaded for money. Hector would gently steer Carlos by them saying, "Don't look at their faces." Carlos had looked though. The watery, bloodshot eyes that met his were empty above the sallow cheeks, whisker stubble, and drool, causing Carlos to shudder.

Anna would say to Hector and Efrain, the oldest two, "Take care of your brothers. Don't let them get hurt by any drunks or anybody in the street." But even if Anna had not said it, Hector would have looked out for Carlos anyway. It was Hector that walked Carlos to school and told him to be careful and not to talk to strangers. It was Hector that helped Carlos ignore the drunks fighting over beer, the fights on the street corners, and the American kids that jeered at them and called them wetbacks. And it was Hector who Carlos looked to for steadfast reassurance that he would be okay in this place.

CHAPTER 9

For there is one God and one mediator between God and men . . . Christ Jesus, who gave himself as a ransom for all men.
(1 Timothy 2:5-6)

New York City was a city of perpetual sound. The street noises were ever present no matter where they lived in the city. Even though Carlos could still see the trains running off in the distance, he couldn't hear them at all in the next place they lived. This place, called the projects, was a lot better and a lot further from 3rd Street. Tio Fernando, Anna's favorite and closest brother, and his Jamaican wife Tina had offered to take them in since their place was slightly larger.

Tina was a very, very clean lady. There wasn't a bad smell or a bug to be found, and Carlos imagined that cockroaches steered clear of the place just because of what they'd heard about Tina. Soon after moving there, Carlos noticed that Tina was fretting over the condition of the bathroom each day. Sure there were six of Carlos' family and five in Tio Fernando's family, so the bathroom did have a lot of traffic. Carlos watched as Tina disappeared into the little room trailing the aroma of bleach and ammonia. "There," she'd say coming out satisfied. But later, she'd be in there muttering and scrubbing again.

Carlos would shrug to Izzy who'd shake his head side to side. Then Tina began eyeing them suspiciously whenever they finished in the bathroom. Eventually figuring out what was happening, she took it upon herself to teach the boys some manners. One day Tina marched the boys into the bathroom.

"You sit down on that thing, don't stand *on* it!" She put the seat down.

"And this is how you sit." She sat. "Number one, you stand; number two, you sit. Now quit getting my bathroom all messy!"

Carlos and his brothers caught on, but before Tina could find fault with any other habits, their stay at Tio Fernando's came to an end. Anna had gotten a job as a seamstress when they first arrived in America so she could provide for her family. Now they were ready to move to their very own apartment—a three-bedroom unit near Crotona Park. Carlos guessed that Johnny may have been right about the opportunities to earn money in this country, but he wasn't ready to accept that having a good-paying job meant a better life.

One day after the move, Hector was feeling sick. Carlos leaned on one of the two sets of bunk beds in their bedroom and tried to make him laugh. He loved to make Hector smile. His happiest times were with his oldest brother. As they talked, Carlos took a close look at his brother in the top bunk. Hector's light skin and angular shape gave the impression that he was a weakling. Watching him laugh, Carlos was overwhelmed by the love that he felt and he wished that Hector's heart was as strong as the bond between them. He worried when Hector tired so easily.

They both paused a moment, sighing after a good laugh, when they heard a door open and excited voices coming from the other side of the wall. "Be right back," Carlos tossed out as he headed for the living

Carlos' mother, Anna, and Johnny

room. His mother was just backing off from an embrace, and Carlos stopped short to see Johnny and Johnny's two daughters standing there, suitcases and belongings at their feet. Carlos' feet seemed stuck to the floor unwilling to move any closer. Izzy and Efrain came to stand beside him and stare. "Now then," said his mother as she brushed past them and steered Johnny towards her room. Johnny, having picked up his valise, gave the boys a smug grin as he let Anna lead him. He had left his wife and followed them to America. Carlos had the sinking feeling that now they'd never go back to Puerto Rico. The sinking feeling rolled around in his gut until his insides felt ravaged. By the time he went back to Hector, Carlos had swallowed the bitter dose of reality and started to feel the strength of renewed hatred for Johnny—the reason they'd left home for America, the one who was the cause of his heartsickness.

Later the extended family of Puerto Rican relatives came by the apartment to greet Johnny and hear how things were back in the homeland. The adults indulged in their meal around the small table while the kids flowed over to stray chairs and the floor in the living room to eat. Momentarily leaving the party, Carlos edged down the small passage to his mother's bedroom. Carlos leaned quietly on the dark, wooden door, pushing slightly with his cheek so that it swung partly ajar.

She had brought all her statues and shrine things from home. Carlos' gaze rested on his mother's bureau. There was her picture of Mary with rosary beads draped across the frame catching the corners as it looped down. Carlos saw that the statues of the saints were set up carefully along the inside edge of the dresser. One saint could speak to the animals; one saint was for healing of disease. Another saint was for prosperity; another for protection over the house. Carlos stood there in the doorway of his mother's bedroom, as if between two worlds. The sounds of visiting came to him from the direction of the living room. The supernatural was displayed poised and ready before him. He wondered if the saints really performed the way they were supposed to, but who was he to know anything? His mother's religious rituals had been passed down for generations and he was just a kid.

Carlos took a small step just over the threshold into the room. He saw big candles, small candles, candles in a glass, and big, fat candles. Off to the side on the wall, was a crucifix of Jesus, and Carlos had heard his mother pray using that name sometimes. He noticed her incense burner. It was a little, steel canister-type of thing with a string and was round and black. Carlos had watched her take it underneath their beds, through their bunk beds, and all around the room. Sometimes she'd go to the Catholic church and bring back holy water to sprinkle on the beds, in the closets, and throughout the apartment. It was a ritual of protection.

Carlos thought for a minute about whether he was comforted by the familiar shrines and rituals of protection. "Too bad," Carlos thought as he turned to leave, "to go through all that and not have it work."

CHAPTER 10

*O Lord, you have searched me and you
know me. You know when I sit and when
I rise; you perceive my thoughts from afar.
(Psalm 139:1-3)*

The three who were chasing Carlos would tear away any part
of his body just to get at his eyes to rip them out. The demons
were fast and strong, and diabolically gleeful in their pursuit of
him through the maze of school hallways. Carlos skidded around
a corner to bolt into the nearest classroom. Feeling the demon's
presence at his back, Carlos fumbled with the doorknob of a stor-
age closet, crying hysterically as he threw it open, jumped in, and
slammed it shut behind him. Tears streaming down his cheeks,
heart pounding, Carlos held onto the doorknob. "Please, please
don't find me!" he begged in a whisper. The sweat of his hands
made the knob slippery to his grasp. Suddenly, the door exploded
into splinters as claws reached to seize him. Carlos screamed and
fought with the might of a pure adrenaline rush, finally escaping
with hanging shreds of clothes, clumps of hair, and great flaps of
skin torn loose from his back. He wondered how he could still be
alive and running with blood dripping from everywhere and hurt
so badly. Still, the demons toyed with his getting away until the
two caught him with exuberant finality. They held him down as
the third plunged his claws into Carlos' eyes to pluck them out.
Carlos screamed—the pain excruciating. And when he could not
bear the pain any longer, he woke up soaked with sweat and
screaming.

Carlos clutched his chest to feel the beat of his racing heart as
he tried to bring his breathing and sense of panic under control.

He must have taken longer than usual to snap out of the awful nightmare, for Efrain in the bunk above him, hissed at him to shut up and quit waking everybody. Carlos ran his hands down the length of bunk bed underneath him. It was real.

Carlos tested rolling his eyeballs around in their sockets under closed lids. He blinked once or twice until the darkened room came into focus. He recognized the shadows of demons moving around him like whispers. He pulled the covers up over his shoulders, mouth, and nose until just his eyes showed. Still the shadows were there. He heard Efrain turn towards the wall and lean close to the edge of the mattress. Carlos knew he wasn't the only one scared of the silhouettes that floated in and around their room. And he wasn't the only one afraid to get out of bed. He closed his eyes listening for the sound of Efrain relieving himself against the wall. When his mother found out, she would give them a beating.

What nightmares did to Carlos during the night, school did to Carlos during the day. It was another morning when Hector waited patiently as Carlos' small hands fiddled unnecessarily with tying shoes over and over again. Carlos stalled on his way to the door as if trying to remember something. He fidgeted with his clothes, gazing intently at a buttonhole, avoiding Hector's eyes. "I hate wearing shoes!" he exploded stooping to undo the laces again.

And then they'd leave the apartment for the streets. Hector would protect him on the way to school, but he couldn't be with Carlos all the time. When they had moved near Crotona Park, Hector would take Carlos to the park and help him fly kites, and Carlos' anger would turn fierce whenever kids made fun of Hector because he wasn't athletic. But in school it was Carlos who was mocked as unacceptable and taunted into worthlessness because he did not speak English.

The school building was cheap-and-plenty-of-it-type brick with the institutional gray mortar that had darkened and camouflaged itself throughout the cinder block foundation. The occasionally-bulged, chain-link fence that surrounded the cracked macadam playground was rusted and dull. Broken glass sparkled from the dirt that separated the playground from the concrete path that faded around the corner to the front of the school building. A fractured, T-shaped sidewalk led to the front double-door entrance that had PS 81 chiseled on a block above it. Walking at Hector's elbow, Carlos tried to match his brother's stride. They parted at the crumbling-cornered steps that led into the school of torment. The warmth of Hector's closeness lingered on Carlos' arm almost until he got to class.

Carlos never knew when he'd get punched or picked on in school, but he knew exactly why. The older boys would come over and put their arms around his shoulders.

"Hey, wetback, what do you have for us today?" they'd guffaw and shove him into one another.

Finally, one of the leaders would take his lunch money. "Twenty-five cents? What an idiot!"

The biggest boy would sneer and slap Carlos in the head. "Idiot!" They'd all murmur in agreement as they each hit him before filtering away down the hall. The girls would laugh at him as he'd stand there alone, humiliated and acutely aware that he was going to be hungry again.

"I am an idiot," he reasoned. "I am Puerto Rican, and I am nothing."

Carlos was miserable. Everything around him was absolutely nothing he had wanted. He had not chosen the situation in which he found himself. He hated everything about the world and the people that were part of this world. The hate he felt was like a drug that dulled his longing to be loved, his need to belong, and his desire to be free of fear. Like savoring sweet dope or swallowing pills whole or shooting lies into one's veins to entice the whole body, little-by-little Carlos became addicted to hate. When an addiction takes over, it feels like strength and control over what causes pain. And Carlos had to stop hurting if he wanted to survive.

So it began; the fight for the right to be something—to be somebody. Carlos had something to prove to people, and it didn't matter who. Young or old, nobody was going to talk him down; nobody was going to call him names. Within the next few weeks, Carlos got mean. Taking a knife to school, Carlos was now ready and willing to cut some kids. He was ready to do anything he needed to do—if it meant cutting them up, then no problem.

"Hold it right there, you little spic. Where do you think you're going without paying?" The boys circled Carlos. Someone kicked him from behind. Carlos pulled the kitchen knife so fast and so fearlessly, ready to slash at the slightest taunt, that almost simultaneously, both the breath and the body of each boy hesitated.

"Hey, come on now, we're not gonna bother you no more, amigo. Honest," said one the boys shrugging his shoulders, palms up in fake resignation. Carlos glared right into the boy's eyes, still psyched up to stab him. Then he saw genuine fear in the boy's eyes and was pleased and slightly surprised by it. Carlos swung around the group. They were starting to back off, the confrontation over. "They are afraid of my anger," thought Carlos. Meanness, hate, and anger would serve him well. "If I hurt others first, I will not get hurt," Carlos decided and put the knife back in his pocket. Nobody was going to take anything from him, not his worth, not his happiness, and certainly not his lunch money.

So Carlos joined those kids at school who had the control, that took the money away from other kids and beat up on those leaving themselves open to attack.

"We know that you're cool, Carlos. You're all right!"

Carlos was an amateur addict when he began the descent into darkness, but soon his habit of hate and anger disguised any fragile remnants of the trusting boy who once lived in a paradise, and Carlos became a hardened user.

Carlos' school picture—about 4th grade and around the time he started taking a knife to school

CHAPTER 11

And Jesus grew in wisdom and stature.
(Luke 2:52)

Carlos learned to fight, he learned to swear, and he learned to steal. There was no reason to steal in Puerto Rico because everything was there. The wild life, the fruit, and the forest were anybody's and everybody's. But life in the city was different and unforgiving.

It had been a hard day at school—at least that's what Preston, a black guy with impressive intimidation qualities, had said. The group of boys shuffled along the sidewalk, threading in and out of parked cars when their bodies together overflowed the curbs.

"Those teachers are so stupid," agreed Edwin as he hacked and spit from between his teeth. He was the same age as Carlos and already the kid had the phlegm of a heavy smoker. Carlos was encouraged. A few more weeks and he'd be able to spit like that.

"Yeah stupid," said Preston as he came to a halt. Following his gaze, Carlos saw the storefront down the street that had caught Preston's eye.

"All grown-ups are stupid," he continued, "they're just too stupid to know it. C'mon!"

They approached the small candy store that was wedged between a deli and a dry cleaner. In the dingy display window to the left of the front door, Carlos could see containers of cellophaned cigars, water pistols and cap guns, and a rack of comic books facing the entrance. Carlos thought of the guys he'd seen sitting on the steps in the neighborhood, chugging their bottles of Yoo-Hoo and backing up their remarks with jabs from a twelve-cent comic book rolled-up to perfection. He silently cursed himself for not having money for the candy store.

"Hold up a minute," Preston was saying, as he elbowed them back.

"You guys wait out here and get ready. Me and him are goin' in."

Preston plucked Rudy, a particularly tough-looking kid, by the shirt as they disappeared into the store. Carlos loitered around with the others outside, pretending not to notice the candy store behind them. Casually he glanced inside. Preston stood directly in front of the counter, talking over it to the owner. Rudy stood behind Preston but slightly to the side so he could reach the shelves just below the counter. Swiftly and without any motion, Carlos saw him slip the crackers and candy into his pocket.

"How much are these?" Preston asked the owner as he held up a pack of cigarettes in front of his face.

"You're too young to have cigarettes," the man said reaching for them. In a flash, Preston threw them to Rudy who threw them out the door to the waiting gang. Preston grabbed a few more items, stuffing and throwing and backing away all at the same time. Roaring with rage, the angry owner charged around the counter to get them, but by then the kids had fled.

As soon as the commotion started, Carlos had begun to run. Preston and Rudy passed him and yelled back to the stragglers to follow them. They skidded around the corner of the block and dashed down a narrow alley that doubled back behind the deli, the cleaners, and the candy store. When they heard the owner still out front in the street yelling, they were overcome with laughter. A smile came to Carlos' mouth without warning as Preston turned to face them running backwards.

"Ha! I told you grown-ups are stupid," he said fairly dancing at the thought of what they'd gotten away with. The rush had gotten to Carlos as well, and it felt good.

A big truck was parked at the end of the alley. It was deserted for the moment and the boys gathered around one of the huge wheels to divvy-up the spoils. Preston shoved Carlos a pack of cigarettes and some candy and Carlos took it.

It was too quiet in the apartment when Carlos got home. He went out to the kitchen to start the beans and rice for the *arroz con pollo*, in case his mother brought chicken home with her from work. He wasn't hungry though. Just then the door to the apartment swung open and his mother and Izzy came in. Carlos came out of the kitchen to meet Anna as she headed back to her room.

"Where have you been?" she accused Carlos but didn't wait for an answer. Carlos watched her shut her bedroom door behind her. Izzy had plopped himself in front of the TV. Carlos came to sit beside him.

"Hector's in the hospital again," Izzy said still absorbed in the show. Carlos felt sick. Putting his hand to his stomach he pulled out a lump from his shirt.

"Here," he said as he dropped a Bonomo Turkish taffy on Izzy's lap. And they sat together watching TV until the daylight turned to dusk, and Gene Rayburn had been replaced by Huntley and Brinkley.

Carlos grew in wisdom and stature; the wisdom of the streets and the stature that finds favor among comrades in crime. He was a quick study when it came to lifting cigarettes from the candy stores. There was usually one owner so there was no problem when Carlos and his friends scurried around the store like ants, opening their clothes to jam stuff in and then run out.

They always went at least four or five blocks down the street, never robbing in their own neighborhood. In their own neighborhood the boys were known, and they didn't want to risk someone recognizing them and calling their parents. It was sort of a code of ethics for them to do their stealing in someone else's neighborhood, and it shielded them from becoming personally responsible for their actions. If the kids didn't know who they were robbing and the victims didn't know them, the theft was of no real consequence. They just didn't care. And that's how Carlos found his way to the rich section of the city.

In the rich section of the city, people didn't seem to worry about crime reaching that far. The children in the houses along the Hudson had clothes, food, and toys enough to lull them into a vulnerable contentment. They'd dutifully park their bicycles in the front yard when they were called in from play, never worrying about loss.

The bus was headed uptown and the boys stood ready. This one had a large enough billboard on the back that at least three of them could stand on the bumper and hold on. The bus slowed for a turn and Carlos and his buddies jumped on. Carlos loved how he could ride anywhere in the city without paying. It was just another freedom that he had come to enjoy, that had been bought by his willingness to wield a knife. Carlos held on to the grimy Lucky Strike advertisement, breathing in exhaust fumes, until the bus came to a stop a few miles away. The boys dropped off the back and nudged each other along the sidewalk, laughing and cursing at nothing in particular.

Carlos saw it first. It was a 3-speed, electric-blue Swenson with chrome handle bars and black handgrips. They stepped off the sidewalk into an overgrown hedge along the far side of the driveway. The bicycle was parked by a small side door off the driveway leading into the house, and Carlos could see several baseball cards attached with clothespins to the spokes of the back tire. "Stupid kid's gonna lose his cards *and* his bike leaving it out like that," Carlos scoffed.

Later, enjoying the bike ride back to the city, Carlos tried to make up his mind what to do with it. He could sell the bike or tear it apart to make a different bike in case the cops came looking for it. Carlos knew better than to keep the body. Maybe he'd just ride it around for a while and then throw it away in an alley somewhere when he got home. It just didn't matter. Nothing mattered.

And then, Hector died.

Hector, shortly before he died

CHAPTER 12

The Lord your God is a merciful God; he
will not abandon or destroy you.
(Deuteronomy 4:31)

No man can contend with one who is stronger than he, and
as much as Carlos proved his strength and defended his worth,
he just couldn't do anything about God. Carlos knew that God
would do good things for you if you were good and bad things to
you if you were bad. And Carlos recognized that he had no
defense against God doing to him what he deserved.

Hector, the brother Carlos loved, was gone. It was a different
kind of gone than when Hector was in the hospital and was just
away from the apartment. Carlos could almost endure the tempo-
rary version of gone. But Carlos hadn't been allowed to see
Hector in the hospital those last days, which was almost like the
real thing. Then, in the end, his mother had refused to let Carlos
go to the funeral, thinking he was too young to handle it. His desperate pleas to attend were dismissed. Hector gone without a
good-bye was like God's punishment for Carlos. Knowing he was
bad was nothing compared to knowing he had been abandoned.

So he gave up on himself, because good or bad just didn't
matter anymore. Carlos thought about his older brother that
remained. Efrain had no fear of anything or anybody. When
Efrain showed up on the street, Carlos could almost smell the fear
rise up from those around him. It was an aroma that Efrain
savored just like Carlos had once savored the smells of Puerto
Rico. Efrain was mean, he was bad, he was tough, and nobody—
not even God—got in his way. Whether someone lived or died,
was robbed, or beat up—it made no difference. If being bad was

the way to survive, then being the toughest was the way to have control, and that's what Carlos wanted. He carried a knife and a lot of hate because he never knew when he'd need a weapon or a reason to handle someone jumping him from an alley.

Carlos' gang formed with about ten regulars, who stuck together to beat up or mug other people. Crotona Park became their territory, their block an unspoken no trespassing zone. If kids would happen by from another neighborhood, Carlos would stand with Preston and say, "This is our block. This is our park. If you want to walk through here you have to ask us permission." The gang enforced their beliefs with fists and violence that didn't lack for use even among themselves.

Carlos and Preston became the gang leaders, but would fight each other to be head honcho. Hours of fighting would go by as, with bloodied lips, noses, and swollen eyes, they'd beat each other until they couldn't swing any more. With knuckles and mouths bleeding they'd call it even. A few months would go by and Preston would declare his leadership. Carlos would immediately challenge him and they'd end up in a fist fight again. When fighting in New York City, a crowd always gathered, which encouraged Carlos a lot. But he could never beat up Preston to the point of winning exclusive gang leadership.

Now, whenever a new kid moved into the neighborhood, Carlos' gang would teach the lessons about who was boss. Membership in the gang required a series of ritual initiations that started with the "donation" of money. Pre-members had to be able to take

Izzy, Maria, and Carlos in New York

what was dished out to them too. But after the beating and judgment on them was passed, they were in. Carlos and Preston enjoyed the relative safety of the gang, but they were not the toughest gang around.

The Trojans were big and had guns and all that. Whenever they had rumbles, Carlos and his friends headed to the roof tops. It was unhealthy to stay in the streets. It didn't matter who you were, staying in the streets meant you'd get trampled down, hit, kicked, stabbed, shot, whatever. Most of the rumbles took place in the school yard, so when Carlos and his gang got up on the roof tops, they could look down in the school yard and see the fighting.

Sometimes rumbles would happen in Crotona Park, right across the street from where Carlos lived. They'd watch the cops come to the edge of the park and just wait. When it was over, the cops would bring in the police transports, pick up the bodies, and take them to the station or to the hospital.

Although Carlos' gang did most of their stealing at night, one time they stole some watermelons from a store in daylight, which Carlos later thought was rather dumb on their part. The owner was a Chinese man and he called the cops on them the minute he suspected trouble. Carlos and the others got the heads-up because they always had a lookout in position. With two cop cars in pursuit, they ran through the schoolyard. Throwing themselves on the tall chain link fence that surrounded the yard, they started climbing. Carlos had been training for moments like these. He was fit and agile as he climbed up, his buddies next to him. The cops drove right up to them but not quickly enough to catch them or to try to scale the fence after them. A whizzing sound flew by close to Carlos' ear and pinged the metal link of the fence as he climbed. More sounds of little darty things whistled by, and Carlos broke out in a cold sweat.

"They're shooting at us!"

Edwin howled and grabbed his leg. The pinging around Carlos continued, and he could hear the cops shouting at them to hold it.

Carlos hauled himself over the top of the fence and landed on the other side ready to take off. Edwin had managed to get over but dropped hard to the ground. Carlos yanked him up and shoved him forward all in one motion. They ran with the yelling and the shooting right behind them. The cops jumped back in their cars and roared down the alley next to the school building. The boys turned a corner in the alley and split up. Carlos dropped and rolled under one of the parked cars. He saw one of the cop cars slowly drive by his hiding place. Carlos centered himself between the wheels. The squad car turned down the next alley, but Carlos lay there for at least an hour until he knew that they were not going to come back around.

Carlos got up all dirty and filthy and scared, thinking, "Man, they were shooting at us. This is ridiculous. We're just kids! Why are they shooting at us?" They had tried to steal watermelons . . . *just watermelons*. His gang was so shaken by the bullets that they gave up stealing by day and, in fact, didn't steal at night for a very long time.

Carlos got a beating from his mother when he got home. It was his shirt that she had been upset about. She let Carlos know that she worked hard for the little money they had to spend on clothes. Carlos peeled off the ripped, dirty shirt before climbing out on the fire escape to smoke.

Shoulder leaning against the rough brick, Carlos lit up and inhaled deeply, considering his gang. His gang wasn't as bad as the big gangs—the ones that were dangerous, hard to get in, and really, *really* hard to get out of. But gangs, after all, were gangs. Each had its share of casualties. Walking to school one day, Carlos had seen a body lying just inside the park. It was covered with blood. The paper read that the victim had been stabbed 22 times. It was nothing to see gang handiwork like that . . . people beat up, knocked out, drunk, or dead. But geez, 22 times! Carlos flicked some ash. No, his gang was not *that* bad.

CHAPTER 13

And the devil, who deceived them, was thrown into the lake of burning sulfur, where... they will be tormented day and night for ever and ever.
(Revelation 20:10)

Carlos approached the building site. He climbed onto the concrete slabs that had been placed on top of each other, the walls unfinished, yet stable enough to support the structure. Carlos investigated, darting around each floor to leapfrog piles of debris and race from one side of the floor to the other. He was goofing around, climbing in and out of the studs, and making shuffling rhythms on the concrete, when he heard a distinct sound from the ground level. Peering over the half-wall where windows were to be, he squinted in the falling darkness into the bottom entrance. Packs of demons were streaming into the building, and Carlos could hear the thuds of their swarming echo through the lower floors. He panicked!

Finding the stairway, he decided he could not go down to get out or he'd run right into them. So he sprinted upward, their yelling and hideous laughter almost snatching the steps out from under his feet. They were coming too fast. The sounds of thudding and rushing were right beneath him now. In desperation Carlos shot through a lone door that led to the roof. Standing there Carlos saw that it was not the roof but the next floor up, unfinished and flat, reaching to the edges of the sky. There were no walls. Moving away from the doorway, Carlos tried to catch his breath. The air held a familiar smell.

Suddenly, demons burst out from the depths of the building, overwhelming Carlos in an instant. He tried to break through their numbers to escape back down the stairs, but the demons grabbed Carlos and carried him over to the very end of the building. They held him dangling out into the void, tormenting him with the threat of dropping him. As some held him, others clawed him, raking their nails the length of his exposed arms and legs. Screaming and fighting their grasp, Carlos thrashed so violently that being punched by Efrain became part of the dream. Efrain shook Carlos again and again, until Carlos became mildly conscious of where he actually was. Carlos inhaled a final trembly breath and knew the smell . . . fear.

Sleep brought nightmares and the setting of the sun brought fear. Carlos was totally afraid of the dark. In the mirrors of his dream world, demons would suddenly appear next to his reflection to drag him into a hell of terror and torment beyond his endurance and with no hope of rescue. In the real world, Carlos began avoiding mirrors, for there was no doubt that he'd see reflections of the demons beside him ready to devour and destroy. No, if he looked into a mirror, Carlos just knew the horrific things he'd see.

PS 92 was a typical junior high. While teachers tried to teach, the students were busy trying on personalities to find which ones would forge the most friendships and which ones secured the best social status. Carlos stayed tough on all fronts. He started lifting weights and worked out regularly. All the running from the cops had made him fast and nearly invincible. At thirteen, Carlos was ahead of most of the kids his age. He was a seasoned shaver, had a talent for dancing (which attracted the girls), and was well versed in the art of street survival. And while he was socially secure with the neighborhood gang, his tight friendships at school provided him a substantial diversion from academics.

His buddies Mintabio and Rudy were leaning against the fence at the far end of the school yard when Carlos and Izzy approached and joined the small semicircle. Shuffling and laughing as they talked, they passed the time until the bell would ring and they'd have to go in. Izzy grew quiet and when the others noticed, he nodded toward Preston emerging from an old Lincoln parked a few yards away. Preston slammed the front car door and exchanged a few words with the driver through his window, then jogged over to join them. Elbowing his way to the center of their group, Preston glanced back the way he had just come.

"Hey, man, what's with you?" Izzy accused.

"Shut up," Preston hissed as he looked nervously around at those standing nearby.

"Look what I have and they're all ours." Preston opened his closed fist, keeping his hand low and within their circle. "Reds. You gotta try these."

No fear. One by one they reached in.

"Nothing to it," Carlos commented as they turned to go into school.

An hour later they were feeling fine, just really fine. Carlos had smiled his way through Math class, feeling smooth and mellowed out. By the time he walked into his next class, he had the giggles. He didn't even care enough to stifle it. The teacher had had enough and sent him to the principal's office. Izzy, Rudy, and Mintabio were already there . . . grinning.

Mintabio and Carlos

The principal looked very serious and was indignant at their offenses and disrespect. He threatened to call their parents and to have them serve detention and tried to make them apologize. But the smilies were upon them, and no threat or explanation would have made any difference. It was all hilarious and they just didn't care.

Yet Carlos did care about one thing, and that was the wonderful discovery of substances that made him feel better. He found out about the drugs that helped him forget the demons in his dreams and in the darkness. He discovered which personalities suited the moment he was in or the girls he was with. He discovered that the amount of drink was proportional to how daring and entertaining the tales told by others were later. And he found out that by crawling out on the fire escape outside of their apartment, he could enjoy a high of choice without fear of the police or his parent.

Another day as Carlos sat in class and watched the teacher write on the blackboard, he started to think ahead to the weekend. He planned to party hearty. If he drank enough to be out of it, he'd be able to handle the night okay. Those were the only times he didn't dream. If he could get stoned enough, there'd be no nightmares for him. Carlos hated when Mondays came and he'd be back at school not knocked out enough to expect to sleep well at night. Every time he closed his eyes, it seemed to signal his availability and the torment of demons plagued him right away.

The teacher was droning on. Carlos spaced out for a while until he sensed someone looking at him. Glancing right, then left out of the corner of his eye, he swiveled around to look at the guy behind him. Instead Carlos looked into the red eyes of a demon staring back at him. The wicked grin implied impending terror and pain. Carlos heard it voice its gravelly threat without moving its mouth. "Just wait—when the bell rings, we're going to get you." Carlos spun around in his seat, stricken. Several minutes passed and he concentrated only on the graffiti etched on the wooden arm of his desk. When he slowly glanced over his shoulder again, no one was there. No one at all.

"Man, Carlos, you're going off the deep end," Preston said when Carlos told him what he had seen and heard.

"It was real I'm telling you!" Carlos defended, but then he started thinking that perhaps he really was going crazy.

"You better quit smokin' and doing all that stuff, man. You're crazier than me," Preston continued as they walked together down the hall.

Carlos knew that eventually the demons would get him and kill him. But in the meantime, the anticipation of his demise made Carlos look for more ways to numb the process and stay longer in that deadened state of mind.

CHAPTER 14

Whoever wants to save his life will lose it, but whoever loses his life for me will find it.

(Matthew 16:25)

The ball games at Crotona Park started at 6 P.M. Armed with large bottles of Colt 45, Carlos and his gang enjoyed the diversion, the brotherhood, and the drink, that when put together was mighty fine. Yet in the drunken darkness after the game, the glass bottles would fly. The joking and faking that started harmlessly enough would always get someone fired up. "C'mon man, don't get mad," they'd try to soothe the insulted one, but sometimes they'd have to resort to punching out whoever it was just to settle him down. Carlos had his share of helping to settle and being settled himself. One time Carlos had been so provoked by one of his gang that he'd broken the neck of a malt liquor bottle and stabbed the kid with it. The kid's coat saved him, but the others had grabbed Carlos and beat him down. When he arrived home with a split lip, his mother had beaten him worse, repeating over and over with each hit, "I told you not to do that! I told you to stay away from those kids!" There were other times when Carlos just didn't go home because, if he had, he knew what was waiting for him.

The gang took care of each other most of the time. After a party, or a fight, when they had the presence of mind, the gang would lay an unconscious member in a building or an open door or something in case of rain. But that kind of care couldn't really be depended on. One time Carlos had partied too much and passed out in the park. Carlos' supposed friends left him and when he came to the next morning, he was stinking, filthy, wet, and alone.

No matter. Unconsciousness was Carlos' peace, for his life was consumed by hate and his sleep was tormented by terror. Carlos stayed awake with the city, going from party to party until exhaustion took over. Several times Carlos stayed awake for forty-eight hours straight because he was afraid to go to sleep. His dreams continued to be so hideous and so real that they scared him to death. He told a few of his friends about the dreams and they'd say, "Man, Carlos, you are one crazy guy. You're going through some weird, weird things, man!"

When the demons would come, it was to tear apart Carlos' body. In his dreams, Carlos would look down at his bones, and his flesh would be shredded and bloodied on them. As the demons clawed him, Carlos screamed, and when the pain was unbearable, he'd wake up. In some dreams, when the demons caught him, they tried to burn him at the stake. They told Carlos of their desire to eat his flesh and take his soul. They wanted to take his spirit and his life. Carlos would stop and look at them declaring, "This is a dream, this is a *dream*!"

"Yes," they'd reply, "but we're still going to kill you."

There were always four or more demons. Two would hold Carlos and the others would just rip at him enough for him not to die, but he always ended up screaming. Twice they tried to throw him off a cliff. Carlos had heard that if you woke up while being killed in a dream, you'd really die. So because he feared for his life, Carlos purposely endured the fall off the cliff and the anticipation of his death as soon as he hit the ground. When he finally awoke, his body would be drenched with sweat.

"You need some pills to knock you out," Carlos' friends told him. So Carlos took the drugs—the uppers and downers that helped him manage his mind. Getting drunk, taking drugs, and going around with his friends added to the transformation in Carlos even more than the dreams, for they had belonged to the confines of sleep hours. But in real life, Carlos was finding his life to be meaningless. He did not care about himself at all—or anybody else. A new thought crossed his mind. "If I kill myself, I'm not going to be able to dream and then they can't get me." At other times in his fourteen-year-old lucid moments, he thought,

"Wow, this is bad for me to be thinking like this. This is not a normal person's thinking. I'm a guy that's together. I've got a gang. I've got people under me. I'm supposed to be together. This is so crazy."

And so it went. Carlos usually didn't care, and it showed at school. The principal would write letters to Carlos' mother about his behavior and academics. Carlos would have to translate them for his mother, for Spanish was all she knew. He was able to keep the truth from her for a while. But when the school provided a different translator, Anna put it all together and came to realize how badly things had gotten with Carlos. The best help for her son would be a spiritist she decided. Anna knew they had power to help the possessed, so she found one not too far from their neighborhood.

Izzy, 12, and Carlos, 14

CHAPTER 15

For the wages of sin is death.
(Romans 6:23)

Carlos stepped into the street as he left his apartment building and gazed down the block. His mother had said that an acquaintance of hers wanted to talk to him. He wasn't convinced he wanted to visit this woman, but the evening was young and her place wasn't far.

When he finally found her door, Carlos knocked hesitantly. She welcomed him in, showing him into her living room. Carlos was tense and began to wonder why in the world he'd let his mother talk him into coming here. But then the lady spoke and said she knew something was wrong with him and that she knew exactly what it was. She told Carlos that he had the Devil in him and that the Devil wanted to kill him. The Devil wanted to snatch his life.

Carlos' nervousness disappeared with her direct words and he thought, Wow, that's exactly right. That's what's happening. Satan's sending his demons to kill me. I can't believe she knows this.

The lady went on. *"Tienes el espíritu de temor.* You have the spirit of fear."

"Yeah . . . *Lo se.*"

"Te van a quitar la vida. They're going to take your life."

"I am . . . afraid, *mucho miedo."* Carlos confessed to her.

"Te van a matar a menos que yo te ayude. They are going to kill you unless you let me help you."

Prompted by her lead, Carlos followed the woman into a small room down the hall from the living room. Candles placed on shelves the whole way around the room flickered as Carlos entered. Immediately a presence took hold of his body.

"Sit down," the lady told Carlos nodding to a single chair in the middle of the room.

With the presence still holding onto him, Carlos felt as if he were walking in the air towards the chair. So strong was the feeling that Carlos looked down as he approached the place he was to sit to see if his feet were still on the floor.

Once he was seated, the woman took a red scarf and put it diagonally across Carlos' chest and tied it. Then she took a green one and tied it across the other way so that together they formed an "X." Satisfied, she tied another scarf over her head and tied it in the back. Carlos thought that she looked as if she were preparing to do battle. Leaning in towards Carlos, she looked him right in the eye and said, "I am going to take everything out of you."

Everything . . . even his very soul? Looking back at her, into her eyes, his heart felt a familiar weakening. He had looked into Abuelo's eyes for smoke and was afraid of what he had seen in them. Now it wasn't smoke but fire that her dark eyes were ablaze with, and total fear washed over him. Every hair on his body was standing up. A cold, cold sweat hit him and trying to rise with her standing right in his way, Carlos said, "I gotta go. I can't do this!"

"Sit down!" she snarled.

"You can't tell me to sit down," Carlos spat back at her. His tough, street-front stance threatened as he stood.

"I'm getting outta here right now so get outta my way!" and he swore.

Abruptly, Carlos was thrown back into the chair. Her hands on him were the claws he had felt in his dreams. Now it was real. Carlos began to shake. Sitting there shaking, scared because of recognizing one of the demons from his dreams, Carlos knew he had to find a way out of this little room.

The woman came around behind Carlos and put her hands on his shoulders. Again Carlos could feel the claws going into him, into his shoulders, and he started saying, "I want to get out of here. I need to get out of here. You need to let me go!"

"BE QUIET!" she commanded him and, just like that, Carlos couldn't talk.

Carlos forced himself to think, to turn over in his mind how to deal with this situation. He couldn't get up because of the strength the woman had on him. But he knew he needed to get away and get away fast. He quieted himself and pretended to give up and cooperate with her. The first chance he got though, Carlos planned to run for it.

The woman started speaking and chanting in a language Carlos had never heard. It wasn't Spanish; it wasn't English. She began to wave some very dried-out branches of some sort all around Carlos as she muttered incantations and appealed to whatever powers she possessed. When she turned around for some other leaves, Carlos saw his chance and bolted from the room.

Dashing to the front door, he found she had locked it securely with three bolts neatly in place. Carlos desperately worked to undo the locks, trembling violently as he heard her coming after him.

"Get back in here! We're not done, get back in here!" she shrieked coming towards him.

"C'mon, c'mon . . ." Carlos pleaded to himself as he fumbled with the door handle. She was upon him just as he threw open the door and made a dash for the street. She followed after him calling and shouting for him until he was too far away to hear her any more.

Carlos found some of his friends and told them, "Man, you got to get me some joints. I gotta get high. I just had a terrible experience!" Good old Mintabio. He always had drugs. Carlos took whatever Mintabio had and got blissfully stoned, forgetting all about the woman, the claws, and the fire in her eyes.

About 3 A.M. Carlos slipped home knowing that everybody would be asleep. Settled in bed he predicted to himself what would happen in the morning when his mother woke up. She'd start in yelling at him and say that he should have stayed there. She'd say something was wrong with him and that this lady would have helped him.

But Carlos really didn't think there was any help for him, for the woman had told him exactly what was going to happen to him.

"They're going to get you; they're going to kill you!"

CHAPTER 16

What a wretched man I am! Who will
rescue me from this body of death?
(Romans 7:24)

Carlos was on his way down, sucked into a spin of party after party, for New York City never slept. The momentum of his drinking and drug use easily kept Carlos going the way he was. He was good-looking. He was popular. And he was possessed—tempted to kill himself to be free from enduring alone against the unexplained mind games and his so-called wonderful life in America.

Carlos walked the street alone, unaffected by the hour or his surroundings. Staying close to the glow from the closed, gated storefronts, he passed few pedestrians before arriving at Mintabio's. Carlos was always informed about where the gang would be hanging out. As long as his supply line to money and a good time held out, they'd continue to be his friends. That was all that mattered really. And when daylight came, they roamed the streets, out of school or out of work, untrained and uncaring.

To his mother Anna, Carlos was growing more and more distant. He had changed so much since they had first arrived, and she felt helpless to combat the badness that she saw in him. In desperation, Anna consulted another of her friends in the neighborhood.

"Carlos! Carlos . . . would you give me a hand please?"

Carlos paused at the bottom of the stairs that led up to his family's apartment. He recognized the nice, little lady that lived on the first floor of their building. With her arms full of groceries, she had come in right behind him and was struggling with her handbag searching for the key to her apartment.

"There's a bag still outside, Carlos. Would you mind?"

"No problem."

Carlos easily lifted the bag from the outside steps. Then taking the bag from his neighbor's arms, he carried them both through the apartment door she held open for him.

"Just go on through and put them on the kitchen counter."

Carlos was just setting them down when he heard the slam of the front door and locks being turned into place with familiar metallic clicks. Carlos had the sinking feeling that he'd been in this predicament before and that he knew exactly what was going to go on.

"Oh man, this is just not real," he swore softly and walked out of the kitchen. For one brief moment they eyed each other.

"I gotta go. I'm not staying here."

"You've got demons in you and I'm going to get them out."

"You need to get out of the way."

"If I don't get the demons out of you, they're going to kill you!"

"I don't care if they kill me, that's fine! Then my life is over and I don't have to worry about this life any more. Now get out of my way, I'm leaving!"

Suddenly Carlos found himself lifted off his feet and carried across the room to a chair. He couldn't believe the strength of this small woman to lift him and throw him into a chair. He tried to get up but invisible chains kept him captive as one by one the hankies were x-ed across his chest.

She took Carlos' hands and rubbed them in a pulling motion, as if she were taking the demons out into her own hands. She threw them out the window and came back again repeating the procedure from the top of Carlos' head down his whole body. Grabbing his legs like a sponge, she pulled and kneaded the demons out and threw them out the door.

"*¿Qué tal te sientes?* How do you feel Carlos?"

"*No me siento nada diferente.* I don't feel any different."

Starting into a whirl of dancing and incantations around Carlos, she grabbed ahold of Carlos, again picking him up with supernatural strength, and shook him. Turning his body around, shaking and commanding the demons to come out, she threw him back into the chair. The realization of an easy out came over Carlos, and he began to play his role in the unfolding drama.

"It's gone, it's gone," Carlos stated like he couldn't believe it himself.

"Yes!"

"I'm free . . . it's gone! I'm free!" he shouted.

"Yes!" his delighted neighbor exclaimed continuing the ritual to be sure. Anna had heard Carlos' voice through the door to the hallway outside the apartment where she had leaned intently listening for any sign that he had been cleansed and restored to her. She turned the knob and went in.

The neighbor lady handed Anna four small vials (all different colors) and said to her, "Boil this in a pot of water and then pour it over his body. Make sure he bathes first." Carlos slowly rose from the chair and made his way toward them. It was over. They would soon be leaving and he'd be out of there.

Arriving home, Anna sent Carlos to take a shower. The water felt good on his body. Carlos closed his eyes and let the spray run over his head and shoulders. He thought nothing; he saw nothing. The sound of the water was soothing and the steam loosened his sore muscles. Turning around he exhaled all the breath and tension that he could push out, and then inhaled deeply through his nose. His eyes jerked open at the awful stench that invaded.

"What the . . ."

"Carlos, I have something that is going to make you better," Anna offered as explanation for the pot of boiling brew that she was about to pour over him.

"Mom! You're *not* going to pour that on me. It's boiling hot . . . I'm going to get burned!"

"This is just herbs and leaves and it's going to cleanse you," Anna pleaded.

"It will burn me!"

Anna paused, then left without further comment and Carlos finished showering. Wrapping a towel around him, he was still standing in the bathroom when she returned. Eyeing each other with the cooled-down pot between them, Carlos finally surrendered to his mother's wishes. Stepping back into the tub, Anna poured the hot, smelly liquid all over Carlos' back and arms and legs. Satisfied, Anna returned the pot to the kitchen and Carlos took another shower just to get the junk off. But the smell had gone into his very pores and would not leave his body.

CHAPTER 17

*I do not understand what I do. For what I
want to do, I do not do, but what I hate, I do.
(Romans 7:15)*

Carlos was sixteen going on twenty-one and messed up on enough drugs to keep a lifetime short. Carlos wasn't worried so much that he couldn't do without marijuana, because it was cheap and easy to get. It was that he needed three or four joints just to get high that bothered him some. Yet Carlos ran a brisk business, selling to kids at school for five dollars a joint, so it wasn't hard to have on hand the stash he needed.

Then Efrain and his friends got hold of some heroin and shared it with Carlos. As the drug had surged through his veins, Carlos began to vomit. He had never felt so sick or thrown up so violently. As he heaved he thought to himself, this is *not* what I want to do. Then as if by magic, he soared so high it was as if jettisoned directly to never-never land. Later his friends recounted how really stupid and arrogant he had gotten, but Carlos could have cared less, unaware of anything that had happened.

Another time when Carlos and his friends had gathered, the pressure was on again to ride that heroin high. Carlos hadn't appreciated the bumpy ride into bliss the last time, but when his friends started clucking at him like some chicken, he could stand it no longer.

"Yeah, let's shoot," Carlos finally agreed. It was all they needed to hear.

Carlos had a conditional kind of leadership among his gang. He was always initiating things to do or ways to party, but he'd always hold off on things he knew were going to end up hurting him. He didn't want to lead the way down the path of heroin use, knowing that he could easily end up a junky. Yet his drinking soothed his nerves and dimmed his resolve. One night at a party, drunk already, Carlos figured he might as well shoot some heroin. He was surprised to wake up in a strange house the next day. Carlos had no idea whose house it was or what he was doing there. Quickly he found his clothes, put on his shoes, and walked out.

Carlos started losing a lot of his memory. His brain cells were becoming too fried. In 11th grade, Carlos finally quit school. At his mother's insistence, he got a job. Carlos was glad for the money since more money meant more purchase power, more pot, more pills, more beer, and more whiskey. The weekends became a cotinuous party, hopping from one place to another, moving along with the whims of his gang and good-time friends. And depression filled his soul; Carlos' life became nothing to him. He didn't care. Again his mother convinced him that a spiritist lady could help him.

This time Carlos was more cooperative because he was so desperate. He thought that if the spiritist lady could help him, he would be glad for it. Carlos cooperated when she gave him instruction. Stand up. Carlos stood up. Put your hands up, she told him. Up went Carlos' hands. She told him to turn around four times. Carlos turned around four times. She told him to speak out the window, so he shooed things out the window. The whole ritual through, Carlos obeyed exactly.

Carlos during his gang days, a prisoner of darkness

Something changed within him, giving way to an unnatural stillness Carlos assumed was peace. Walking home when the spells were through, Carlos thought perhaps he was better. That very night, his last waking thought was that the happenings of that day were good, and the incantations of the spiritist had truly tamed the evil spirits that haunted him. Then he fell asleep into the most horrifying nightmare of his life.

He knew he was sleeping—dead but awake. Carlos gazed down at his stomach and saw worms, hundreds of them, crawling and writhing up out of his stomach. Worms squirmed from the tips of his fingers and from each part of his body. Carlos knew he was dead and that his body had begun to decay. The maggots and worms consumed his body as he lay there and watched it happen. His chest was covered with them now, and he filled his lungs to cry out. The legless white grubs twisted and wriggled with his chest's movement, and they slid and nestled into his armpits. Finally with a lung full, he screamed himself awake and then violently trembled until the sweat had dried on the hairs of his body, cold and sticky against his flesh.

Then things got worse. A hatred for his mother began to fester within Carlos. He reasoned that Anna had no right to subject him to all this weirdness. Each new day the nightmares, the evil spirits, and the drugs drove Carlos into anger and hate and madness, and he was prisoner to them. Carlos had no idea where it all was coming from but knew he could no longer live with Anna's solutions or her response: "They're just dreams, Carlos. Don't worry about it."

Finally his imprisoned spirit became a physical reality when Anna, after taking him to breakfast one morning, turned Carlos in at the local precinct. Now he was truly incarcerated. As the doors swung shut, Carlos' hate for his mother grew even more and he shouted at Anna, "What am I doing here? How can you do this to me, your own son?" In that two-week period, being physically beat up in prison did nothing to deter the remote hardness that encased Carlos' soul.

Carlos was lying in a bunk in the cell for four, when the jailer came by with a list. Carlos heard his name called.

"Did you say Carlos Rivera?" Carlos asked through the bars. "My name is Rosado, but my mother's name was Rivera."

"Yeah well, are you Rivera?"

"Uh yeah . . . I'm Rivera."

"Alright, get out."

In short order, Carlos was looking across a desk at a judge. Peering occasionally over the top edge of the papers in his hand, the judge inquired, "Did you learn your lesson?"

"Yes sir."

"Are you going to quit the drugs and stay straight?"

"Yes sir. I'm not going to do that stuff ever again."

"Alright. You're free to go."

Anna arrived home from work that evening. She hadn't expected to find Carlos sitting in the living room, watching television, unmoving, detached, and solemn.

"What are you doing here?" she asked.

"I escaped from prison. I go where I want, I do what I want, and nothing can stop me."

CHAPTER 18

For God so loved the world that he gave his one and only Son, that whoever believes in him shall not perish but have eternal life.

(John 3:16)

Carlos had some time to kill. He didn't feel like doing much of anything, for summertime in the city brought on laziness tinged with boredom. He had long forgotten how to enjoy or care about the world around him and the things that used to make him happy. Even the short time Carlos had lived with his girl-friend after getting out of jail hadn't cured the man he had become. Now he was just sitting on the stone steps to his apart-ment building, smoking and watching the perpetual traffic go by.

A girl came down the sidewalk. Carlos, intent on his ciga-rette, expertly flicked ash and poised the butt to take another drag. He sized her up from the corner of his eye as she approached. Pretty. Somewhere a radio blared. She paused briefly to look at Carlos and then started up the stairs past him into his building.

"Jesus loves you," she said quietly to Carlos. Carlos let out a grunt and squinted at her through the smoke he had just exhaled.

"Jesus loves me? Ah . . . I don't think so." Who did she think she was, this girly looking so fine and speaking to him like he cared about anything coming out of her mouth? His look and his curse words followed her inside. Later she was back, coming out through the doors and right by him. She looked Carlos right in the face and smiled.

"I mean it, Jesus loves you."

"*Ojo m'ija!*" Carlos snapped at her. "You don't even know me. You don't know who I am, so get out of my face before I slap you," and he cursed her out again.

She came back the next day, and Carlos happened to be sitting in the same spot smoking cigarette after cigarette.

"I want you to know, Jesus loves you."

"Well I want *you* to know I hate Jesus. I hate God. God took my brother, God took my life, and I hate God. I hate religious people too. They're nothing but a bunch of hypocrites. I hate them and I hate you so don't keep telling me that Jesus loves me!"

But Naomi did—every time she came to visit her father living in the same apartment building as Carlos' family. And each time it seemed that Carlos was hanging out on the steps, guarding his turf, smoking his unfiltered Camels, and getting angrier by the minute.

"Jesus loves you," Naomi would say. Carlos would curse in return and spit out every put-down about God and religion and anything else that he thought would make her quit handing him that same unbelievable line every time she went by.

After a couple of weeks, Carlos had reached the end of his patience. When Naomi arrived to go up and visit her father, Carlos spoke first.

"Don't start with me girl. Telling me that Jesus loves me is such a lie! I'm sick of hearing you say it."

Naomi smiled. "Why don't you come to church with me?"

"Church? Oh man, I hate church! I hate church people! And go anywhere with you? I hate everything about you, so quit buggin' me."

Naomi was just about to move away with a shrug and a smile, when a man around Carlos' age strolled up the steps to join Naomi and Carlos. Carlos thought he had seen him around but couldn't quite place where.

"This is my brother Henry," Naomi said.

"Oh yeah?" Carlos tossed aside his unfinished smoke and stood. Carlos moved directly in front of Henry, solid and menacing. About Carlos' size but not quite as muscular, Henry didn't step away, his gaze remaining even, his stance unthreatened by Carlos' invasion of his space. This guy doesn't even know how close he is to getting beat up, thought Carlos. How stupid can he be?

Naomi looked from one to the other and sensed Carlos' unspoken challenge.

"Henry knows karate," she offered.

"Karate? You know karate?" Carlos said to Henry.

"Yeah..."

"Yeah, right. Show me something then." Carlos jumped away, prancing and chopping at the air while making obnoxious sound effects like the 'Hai Karate' aftershave commercials. Henry laughed.

"Come at me like you're going to attack," Henry baited Carlos and gestured with his hands.

Carlos immediately came at Henry, fist raised and ready to strike with the switchblade that had sprung from nowhere. Easily, Carlos found himself looking up at the sky from the hot, dirty sidewalk, thinking how glad he was that none of his gang was around to see this. He got up and came at Henry again. Again he was downed. Henry's smiling face came into view above him.

"Black belt," was all he said.

CHAPTER 19

Come near to God and he will come near to you.

(James 4:8)

Free karate lessons. No problem. Carlos was an excellent athlete, and learning karate was something Carlos just soaked up. So much running from the cops made him fast. Gang fights and intramural boxing made him agile and strong. But karate put him among people that hadn't seen either. At first Carlos didn't put much stock in Henry's toughness, but during lessons he saw a confidence in Henry that implied unyielding power and strength.

As Henry and Naomi spent time with Carlos and worked on their karate together, Henry would talk of God. It was mostly simple stuff like Naomi had started with Carlos. You are loved. Someone cares about you and how you're doing. Carlos brushed it off. Listening to this stuff was the price he'd pay to be able to fight off any attack of an enemy. Carlos liked the feeling he got when he trained toward something physical. It wore him out and diverted his attention.

"Come to church with us," Naomi tried again one Saturday afternoon. Carlos had been trying to impress Henry and Naomi that he was a together kind of guy, good at karate, good at managing his life, and good enough that church was no big deal. He wasn't afraid to go and thought perhaps it would be nothing, like going to school or stopping by a store. What was so threatening about church?

"Yeah, okay, I'll go."

They came by early the next morning in a bus from the chapel. Carlos was lying in bed. His mother came in and shook him awake. "They're here from church to pick you up."

Carlos rolled on his stomach with a moan. It had been a late night of partying. "Tell them I'm not here."

Anna went to the window and yelled out to the street. "He's here in bed!"

The next thing Carlos knew, Henry was standing beside him, ready to drag him out of bed if needed.

"Oh, man! I don't believe you . . . just come in a guy's house to take him to church! Man, you're some piece of work," Carlos grumbled on and on as he pulled on the muscle shirt he'd worn the day before and some shorts. Sliding his feet into sandals, he followed Henry out to the waiting van and rode, half asleep, all the way to the chapel.

The chapel, at one point, had been an old roller skating rink. It was only about twenty by forty feet, though, so it wasn't very big. When Carlos walked in, the first thing he noticed was the back of the heads of some of the ladies there. They had small white pieces of cloth covering their heads. It was unlike the veils or scarves that the women would throw over their heads when entering the Catholic church his mother went to. In fact, Carlos was transported back to his Puerto Rican memories of using little white pieces of material like theirs to catch guppies in the river. And here they were on their heads! Carlos looked around and shook his head. This was some kind of wacky, wacky place.

Almost at the same time he entered the chapel, people there noticed his arrival and came to greet him. Some hugged him; others clapped him on the back. But each one used his name and a lot of enthusiasm.

"Hi, Carlos!"

"Hey Carlos, so glad you could make it!"

"Great to see you here, Carlos!"

And Carlos thought, Man, where do these people know me from? How do they know anything about me?

By the time Carlos left the church, his head was spinning with the craziness of it all. The people had been so interested in him, like they genuinely cared for him. They hadn't wanted his money. They hadn't wanted anything from him. They were just so glad he was there.

Riding home in the church van, Carlos thought about the strange morning. They had hugged him—physically hugged him—and it surprised Carlos how good it felt. Even now he still felt their embrace and not only physically. They had looked forward to his coming and were filled with joy, a real happiness, when they were all together. Carlos had sensed a presence there that had rested on him within the place. It was peace. Complete and profound peace. It had been wonderful and great, and Carlos had been reluctant to leave.

The minute Carlos walked back into his family's apartment, a dark weight came upon him. "Glad to have you back," the evil spoke to him. "Don't give those peculiar people another thought," the presence assured him. Carlos couldn't begin to explain to himself why he suddenly felt uncomfortable in his own home, but the feeling of not belonging there was even stronger than when they'd first come to New York. It was a different sense of not belonging, and Carlos said something to Naomi and Henry the next karate lesson they had.

"It's the spirit of God in you," Henry pointed out.

"God? In me? Hey, I got spirits but it ain't no spirit of God— I can tell you that right now."

But Naomi and Henry continued to explain and talk to Carlos about how much God loved him. They told him that nothing he could do would get in the way of God loving him.

CHAPTER 20

I will give you a new heart and put a new spirit in you; I will remove from you your heart of stone . . .
(Ezekiel 36:26)

Carlos was standing on the small bridge over the lake watching some little kids drown. As a member of the lifeguard team at Camp Brookhaven in the Catskill Mountains, Carlos had told those kids that if they couldn't swim, they shouldn't jump in. They'd jumped in anyway and Carlos thought it served them right to let them drown. Carlos just watched them floundering and thought, I'm not going in after those kids.

Everyone was yelling at Carlos, "Go get them! Go in and get those kids!" Pausing a moment longer to conjure up some pity, Carlos finally dove in and pulled them out. Pressing their little bellies full of water, Carlos worked on them until they quit coughing and spitting out water.

"I told you kids not to go in there. If you go in there one more time, I'm not going in after you."

A mean streak hit seventeen-year-old Carlos that summer. He had always been a good swimmer—from the days on the river in Puerto Rico to life guarding at the Crotona pool in the city. But he had no patience for the camp kids that seemed to drown themselves on purpose. Carlos couldn't wait for the week of teen camp. He would have no problem going in to save pretty girls. I'll let the rest of the kids drown, but save only the pretty girls, thought Carlos to himself. But it didn't work because pretty girls didn't want to get their hair wet and never jumped in. No, it did not work that way at all. And the mean streak continued the more Carlos tried to balance his double life.

Carlos had spent a lot of time hanging around that weird little church, Fellowship Chapel. Carlos had found a warm, accepting place among the church people. They wanted nothing from him, so he knew their care for him was genuine. He felt a peace there that had eluded him from the moment his family had moved from Puerto Rico to the city. Within the few weeks of getting to know pretty Naomi and her brother Henry, Carlos had felt comfortable enough to go with them to this camp and help out. Yet he kept his fun life in reserve just in case he needed a really good time.

Carlos

Carlos loved to party and especially loved to dance. He was good at dancing and the girls wanted to be with him. He felt desired, which was a powerful thing for any strong, good-looking guy. Yet, his pursuit of a good time with his street friends was tempered by wanting to know what he was missing at church. It was getting more and more confusing to him to figure out what a good time was. So Carlos sat there on the bridge in the sun, watching the kids and wishing for a cigarette to help him think straight. Why couldn't he have his life both ways? Why was a choice looming before him?

He thought back to his uneasy walks through Crotona Park to get to church without his gang finding out. Occasionally he'd run into some of his friends. Carlos would quickly take the small New Testament from his front pocket and stuff it in a back one before they got too close.

"Hey, Carlos my man. Are you ready to get high?" Mintabio would sling an arm around Carlos' shoulders and flash a knowing smile.

"Not right now . . . I've got to do something for my mom." Carlos would try weakly. He sort of missed the guys in the hood.

"Hey, c'mon man," Preston encouraged. "What's the matter with you, Carlos? You're not yourself, man."

"Uh . . ." Carlos weighed the decision briefly as they stood around him expectantly.

"Okay, let's go."

So they'd set out to score before heading to where the party was gathering. And Carlos would get high with them—but not so high that he didn't know what he was doing. And Carlos would enjoy a drink with them, but his laugh never reached his eyes, and he'd pour his beer on the ground when they weren't looking. Preston was right. He wasn't himself.

CHAPTER 21

But God demonstrates his own love for us in this: While we were still sinners, Christ died for us.

(Romans 5:8)

One night during camp, Henry told Carlos about revival services that were being held back at Fellowship Chapel in the city.

"Carlos, you should go."

"No . . . *you* should go. You like revivals. You're a holy guy, you'd enjoy it."

"C'mon Carlos. You should go."

"Aah, I don't know if I want to go."

Henry paused a moment and considered Carlos. He had told Carlos of God and His love for him. Yet while Carlos had heard Henry's words and had seen his life, there was still a weighing going on within Carlos. And no amount of talk could undo a past, release a prisoner, or convince a heart. Henry decided to take advantage of Carlos' weak spot.

"Listen, Carlos. Several of the service workers here from Pennsylvania really want to go down. Won't you go with these girls just to keep them company?"

Carlos thought about being in a car with girls for the two-hour drive down and back. Any time spent in the company of females was fine with him.

"Oh alright," he agreed.

It felt familiar and good sitting there in that roller rink chapel in the city. It was crowded but happily Carlos was wedged in between two of the girls he'd ridden down with. Carlos loved the music and the good feeling he got from the people and the songs that swirled around him, boosting his mood. As they were seated, a small man stood and preached to the crowd. Carlos had heard Pastor Hill before, so he just sat there in the service and let his mind wander. He was here wasn't he? He didn't have to actually listen to the guy.

Carlos thought about Henry and Naomi and the people at the church. He knew he felt good around them, but he didn't want to take that next step, to take to heart what they were telling him about hope for a future. Carlos knew feelings changed depending on the people around you or the drugs in you. High or hateful, pleasure or painful—it was all about circumstances, not choices. Yet when he was with these people, his happiness matched theirs, and there was something genuine about it. Carlos glanced down at his hands. Sitting there among them now, he felt like a fake. Nobody else knows I'm a fake, Carlos thought, But I know I'm a fake. He sighed and decided he couldn't trust his feelings at all.

At first he wasn't listening. He was still thinking. But he did, in fact, hear the word *cross*, several times. Carlos looked up. He couldn't make sense of what Pastor Hill was preaching, but Carlos heard him saying something about the Cross of Jesus. Carlos thought to himself, There has to be something different. There has to be more to this life than what I have. The Cross of Jesus. Carlos carefully examined himself, tempted to back away from God in guilt, yet drawn to the glimmer of hope in becoming free from all in his life that held him prisoner. The Cross of Jesus. I am so messed up, thought Carlos. Sin. I'm so full of it that I don't think I have what it takes to be good.

The girl next to Carlos began to cry. Carlos glanced around and noticed some people had gone up to the front of the church. He heard Pastor Hill repeat an invitation to come forward and thought, This girl needs to go up front.

"Do you want to go to the front?" Carlos whispered gently to her.

"Yes," she nodded wiping her eyes.

Carlos stood to let her pass by. As she left her seat, she pushed him along ahead of her until they were both in the aisle, side by side. A collective, pleased murmur washed over them as she took Carlos' hand and led him forward to the altar. Carlos knelt down next to her as she continued to cry. Carlos was aware of a few others that gathered around them. When the girl reached up and placed her hand on his left shoulder, Carlos was amazed at the feeling—like nothing he'd ever felt before. And she began to pray.

"Lord, I pray for Carlos."

What is this, Carlos wondered? Was this girl crying and praying for *him*?

"Lord, I pray for Carlos. Lord, save Carlos and come into his heart."

Another voice joined in, and another, all praying for him. *All praying for him!*

Carlos could feel their hands upon him. They prayed as if they loved him. And Carlos suddenly knew, really *knew* that God indeed loved him too. He was filled with the wonder of it. Carlos started to feel his whole left side leave his body. It felt as if it were being lifted, going up and up. It was such a strange feeling of being separated—like being torn in half. Pastor Hill joined the little group and placed his hand on Carlos' right shoulder.

"Bring salvation to Carlos' heart. Let Jesus come into his heart and set him free."

Carlos felt his whole body start to float upward. With his eyes closed, Carlos marveled at the sensation. He hovered so far up he thought his head would hit, knowing how small the altar was and how low the ceiling was. He opened his eyes to look up and see the

Fellowship Chapel in the Bronx

ceiling. It was still up there and looking down Carlos discovered his knees still on the carpet. An overwhelming presence came into him so powerfully that he could not help but weep at what was revealed.

The Cross was before him—placed there in love for him. Now the time had come for Carlos to decide what he was going to do about that Cross. God's love for him had always been there, just waiting for him to accept it. So Carlos took all the bad, all the hurt, all the sin—not just part, but all of it—and nailed it to the Cross. The Cross of Jesus. Could one so bad be forgiven so completely? Carlos let go then and cried to God.

"Lord, I need you right now. God, come into my heart!"

And God did. For Carlos' sin, every last bit of it, was nailed to the Cross, and Carlos never again would have to bear the weight of it. Carlos was free.

"Lord, however you work—I don't know what to say, I don't know how to pray—just whatever you need to do, do it. Jesus, forgive me for my sins. Clean my heart and make me a new person."

For the first time in his life, Carlos felt clean and whole and new . . . so new. God's forgiveness completed him, and he knew he would never again have to face this life alone.

CHAPTER 22

Your word is a lamp to my feet and a light for my path.
(Psalm 119:105)

Carlos struggled to understand the Bible that Henry had given him. The drugs and the dope had scrambled his brains so much that he couldn't understand anything he read. In school Carlos had struggled with reading. If education included knowledge of ways to give teachers a hard time, Carlos would have excelled. And rather than literature comprehension, Carlos had been educated in street survival skills. The frustration of not making sense of the words and what they meant did nothing to help what was happening to Carlos back in the real world—his world.

"Henry . . . I'm done. I can't do this." Carlos threw the Bible at him. "I'm not going to make it as a Christian."

The old gang had found out that Carlos had religion now and their harassment was merciless. "Oooo, here comes Holy Joe," they'd cat call as Carlos came down the street. They'd gather around and throw cheap shots that knocked him off balance. Carlos took the hits and the slaps they jabbed at him.

"Hey, you're not supposed to hit back, right? No hitting back goody-goody!" they'd taunt and hit him some more. Inside him anger boiled to the brink. Carlos clenched his fists. Here were kids that he had easily beaten up, that had been afraid of him, and now they were his fearless tormentors.

"I'll help you read the Bible, Carlos. I will, man. You gotta hang in there," Henry would reply but Carlos was too disillusioned and illiterate to be encouraged.

Carlos was also finding it increasingly hard to live in his own home. Just walking into the apartment, his brothers and cousins would mock him.

"You know Carlos, you're an idiot. Religion is for the weak, man. You're a weakling now. That's what people around here think. Man, everybody hates you, you're stupid." The talk was constant and humiliating.

"I can't take this. I don't know if I can keep going like this," Carlos would tell Pastor Hill at the chapel. Carlos would listen to all the godly words the pastor would share with him. His advice and his wisdom would bolster Carlos' resolve to go back home and live a good Christian life despite it all. But Carlos would fail and a warped reasoning invaded his thoughts.

"I'm just not good enough and maybe God just doesn't love me enough. If God loved me, I'd be more like Henry. But I'm not and never will be. I'm not going to make it."

To make matters worse, the dreams and nightmares continued, coming sometimes three and fours times in one night. There was no rest at night . . . ever. Carlos carried his tiredness to the spot welding job he had during the day. Eventually, his continually falling asleep on the job gave the foreman cause to fire him. Mintabio heard about it.

"I told you this stuff is just hocus-pocus, man," Mintabio said. "These people are not for real. It's all about rituals and money and they're not in the real world. You don't need that, man."

"Yeah, I probably don't need that. I don't need that at all." Carlos agreed.

Efrain invited Carlos to a birthday party at his place. It was big and all of Efrain's gang and hook ups were there. Carlos drank the night away and was more miserable than ever. Another party and Carlos was stoned again. Carlos went through all the familiar motions, but something wasn't setting right with him. Hanging around with his old friends was not feeling as good as he thought it used to. What happened to me? he thought. What happened to all that good stuff?

Carlos stood on the steps that led into his apartment building, smoking and watching the cars go by. That was where Henry found him again. The look that exchanged between them said it all. Carlos' eyes betrayed his weariness and Henry's his sorrow.

"Carlos, give it one more chance. Don't give in! Just one more chance."

Carlos blew out smoke and threw his cigarette on the ground. He pulled up his collar against the chill November evening, all the while deciding—deciding what to do.

"Okay Henry. One more chance, that's it."

"I want to pray over you. I want to lay my hands on you and pray for you."

"Right here?"

"Let's move just inside to be warmer."

They turned toward Carlos' apartment building together and there inside the entrance, Henry prayed. Placing his hands upon Carlos' head he said, "Lord, give Carlos a new brain. Give Carlos an understanding of Scripture." Carlos received Henry's words like a gift right to his heart.

"Yes Lord, that's what I need!"

In the morning Carlos reached under his mattress for the

Carlos at Fellowship Chapel, several months after Henry prayed that God would give Carlos a new brain

Bible Henry had given him. Opening it to the book of John, Carlos read. It was as if the light of day were showering down on him. He read that from the very beginning, God loved him. It was so clearly there: God *loved* him. Carlos read. In the beginning God cared for him and he was God's child. The words on the page became alive and Carlos could not put the Bible down. So Carlos read and read, memorizing and storing away Scriptures into his newborn mind.

To encourage Carlos, one of the men at church gave him a devotional book to read. Carlos opened the book and started to read but couldn't make any sense of the words. He tried to read another recommended book that would help him grow, but still he could not understand it. For the year that followed Henry's prayer, the Bible was all Carlos could read. He just could not put it down, reading at every opportunity, no matter where he was.

CHAPTER 23

It is for freedom that Christ has set us free.
Stand firm, then, and do not let yourselves
be burdened again by a yoke of slavery.
(Galatians 5:1)

The dreams were intensifying and Carlos felt like sleep had become his battle ground. The demons that plagued him, no longer went for his eyes but rather his throat. The choking was awful and each time Carlos struggled for his life. The demons seemed to take turns. Once they caught him, one demon would choke him until his strength ebbed, then another would take his place. There were so many of them and Carlos could take it no longer.

Leaving the apartment about 9:30 one Friday night, Carlos made his way to Fellowship Chapel. Pastor Hill answered his insistent knock.

"Pastor, I'm at a crossroad here. I cannot take what is going on at home. I can't take the drinking, the cursing, and the dirty movies. I just cannot take the evil going on at my house. And if I don't stay here, I might take the worst turn ever in my life."

"You'll be okay, son. Sleep here tonight." Pastor Hill opened the chapel door wide and relieved, Carlos entered.

It was almost midnight and Carlos was awake. He looked up from the couch at the shadows on the ceiling. Light must be coming in from somewhere behind him. Carlos got up. The chapel's office door was ajar, and street lights from outside were filtering in through the small, office window. Carlos pushed the office door open. A shaft of light fell across the desktop. It was Friday—payday—and stacks of money used to pay the staff at Fellowship

Carlos at 20, ready for Voluntary Service in San Francisco where he met Ruth, his future wife

Chapel were in orderly piles, awaiting distribution.

Carlos stepped closer. Look at all this money . . . piles and piles. I could take this money and leave New York and never come back. How he wanted to leave, to save himself, to free himself from the burden of his life here. Carlos put his hands on the bills a moment, then walked back to the couch and lay down.

How far could he get with that money? What could he do? What could he buy? Carlos got up. He grabbed a stack of bills and flicked them through his fingers like a deck of cards. He counted the pile. Sixty dollars. Another stack had twenty. He lifted a bundle to his nose and inhaled. Savoring the scent, he continued to count—this stack, fifty; another stack, one hundred. Oh man! Carlos went back and lay down.

Without intending to, Carlos drifted off into dreamless sleep, unaware that money would never be the reason for his freedom. And as the sun rose over Fellowship Chapel the next morning, Carlos woke up to find the payroll intact, and his buried feelings of unworthiness, unacceptability, and sin-sickness still yoking him to his past.

In the testimony of Carlos' young life, the battles

Ruth and Carlos

weren't really against flesh and blood, even though Carlos wouldn't realize that until a few years later. For right now, Carlos knew that God had His hand on him, and no matter what the temptation, Carlos could remain assured that God would keep him in the depths of His love and cover times of weakness, fear, and doubt with His power, His presence, and His truth.

The circumstances surrounding Carlos' life changed frequently over the years, things often happening over which Carlos had no control. But never, ever again would he feel alone, abandoned, or beyond God's forgiveness—for God knows Carlos and He calls him by name.

PART THREE

The Battleground
1996-1998

"Dear heavenly Father, I ask You to reveal to my mind now all the sins of my ancestors that are being passed down through family lines. I want to be free from those influences and walk in my new identity as a child of God. In Jesus' name, amen."

The Bondage Breaker—Neil T. Anderson

Chapter 24

For our struggle is not against flesh and blood, but against the rulers, against the authorities, against the powers of this dark world and against the spiritual forces of evil in the heavenly realms.
(Ephesians 6:12)

"Have you ever been involved in the spirit world?" asked the special speaker one evening at a spacious church in Mechanicsburg, Pennsylvania. Now middle-aged, married with four children, and employed with the Buckeye Pipeline Company, Carlos sat there in the church so different from the little Fellowship Chapel in the Bronx. Though he did his best to live as one redeemed by the blood of Jesus Christ, Carlos found himself often surrendering to anger, nightmares, and demonic fears that interrupted his life without warning. He had learned to generally just accept that this was the way it was for him, but the question presented that night began to rattle the spiritual chains that still bound him.

"If you have been prayed over by a spiritist, had a relative who practiced witchcraft of any kind, or have been cursed, come up to the front of the church."

Suddenly it all made perfect sense. The statues, the incantations, the ritual cleansings, and the supernatural visitations that were his childhood past, were a part of him still. Although Carlos had long ago nailed his sins to the Cross of Jesus Christ, the deceptions of the enemy, and the ancestral sins of his family, had kept his soul a battleground far too long. It was time to seek help from the One that had already won the war.

Carlos answered the question by going forward. Together with the pastors and the deacons, they prayed. With a warm hand on Carlos' head, the minister rebuked and renounced every hold on Carlos that had been spiritually passed down to him from the generation before. And at this altar, as at that first little altar in the Bronx, Carlos was flooded with God's love for him—only this time he knew exactly how he would pray.

"I rebuke and renounce the Devil's stronghold on me, in the name of Jesus. Take all these evil influences out of me. Lord Jesus, I surrender myself to you!"

At the utterance of those words, Carlos fell to the floor unconscious, later to wake up ready to strike out against the spiritual forces of evil. Yet, the ones yoked to Carlos for so long would not give up their strongholds in him easily. It wasn't long after his surrender, though, that God was faithful to remove the blinders from Carlos' spiritual sight. By God's grace, Carlos could fearlessly look straight into the eyes of the enemy and anticipate the fight.

Settling down in their bed together one night, Carlos and his wife Ruth had just started to drift off to sleep. Their children had already been put to bed each in their own rooms. Suddenly, Carlos heard footsteps running toward their bedroom.

"Daddy!" sobbed their young daughter Angie as she leaped in the darkness for their bed. Carlos could feel her trembling as Ruth stroked her hair.

"What is it, darling?"

"Something..." Angie whimpered, "Something ran into my room under my bed!"

Carlos threw back the covers and walked down the hall to Angie's room. He paused at the doorway. It was not easy to see depth in the darkness, to tell what was real or illusion. Why did this feel familiar to him?

The bed shook slightly as Carlos sat down and began to pray. He listened to his own voice as he prayed aloud battling the unseen enemy. How different this fight was from the one around his own bed so very long ago. But unlike his mother's battle against demons, Carlos knew exactly who he bowed down to— the true and only power that could prevail against such an enemy.

"By the power of the name of Jesus, I command you to leave this room. In the name of Jesus, leave this room!" Carlos ordered.

Immediately, the hair on Carlos' legs stood up, and with a mighty rush, something darted out from under the bed and flew from the bedroom. Carlos felt the presence go right by his legs on its way out the door. Filled with God's Spirit and praising the Lord, Carlos walked back down the hall to his waiting wife and daughter, with all the confidence and authority that a child of God should have.

Chapter 25

Submit yourselves, then, to God. Resist the devil, and he will flee from you.
(James 4:7)

Carlos' gift of spiritual discernment grew. He became involved not only in the prayer and healing ministry at the church but also with the youth. When he reached out to the teens, he was energized and passionate about sharing that marvelous message of hope and forgiveness. Carlos felt blessed just being with them.

There would be times when Carlos sensed a hurt that no one else would know about and was often able to see when problems in the home were connected to the spirit world. Carlos sought the Lord on behalf of others, and God would reveal to Carlos how to pray for them. He thrived in his calling and looked for every opportunity to get closer to the heart of God. It was not so very odd then, that the closer Carlos grew to God, the more something within him felt unresolved. Was his soul battle really over?

Carlos had just gotten off work and regret was already rising up in his mind as he drove home. In obedience to God's prompting, Carlos had called Pastor Ken and a few others at the church and made arrangements for a special time of prayer for whatever it was that he needed to settle in his spirit. Carlos knew he could be open and honest with the prayer warriors that were coming together and that was good. His regret, however, was in the expectation that something in him would drastically change because of this meeting. And he just didn't feel ready to dig up anything that might have been buried and covered over for a long time.

Meanwhile, God recognized His own when the call for help came to Him in the heavenly realms. As the earthly saints began to fast and pray for Carlos during the week before this scheduled meeting, extra measures of spiritual strength and discernment were sent with the unseen angelic forces that had begun to gather at the battle sight. With their approach, the enemy was alerted and Baanah immediately went in search of the demonic spirit that had resided in the likes of Virginia so long ago in Puerto Rico.

Usually Carlos looked forward to these times of intercessory prayer that always started with the praise and worship of God. But as Carlos came through his front door from work, another powerfully subtle entity blew into Carlos' thoughts along with the spirits of regret and oppression. Manohar (one who wins over the mind) suggested to Carlos that calling together all these people to pray for him was a waste of time. He didn't really need it, did he? After all he was a *righteous* guy.

Changing out of his work clothes, Carlos got into the shower. Closing his eyes, he let the spray run over his head. The sound of the water was soothing. But as the water ran down his back, Carlos felt something else too. A hand . . . Carlos felt hands rubbing his back.

"Carlos, *hijo* . . . it's Virginia. Don't worry, I'm going to take care of you like I used to," the spirit lied. "You don't need to have prayer. I will take care of you."

Carlos leaped out of the shower and ran to his room to grab his clothes. Putting them on as he went, he felt the demonic presence following him. In his rush to the car, his movements became stronger, more purposeful, and defiant. Flinging open the door of his Grand Am, it seemed as if the presence overtook him, and he started to feel more powerful and mean than he had in years. Turning the ignition key, he reached up on the dashboard for his sunglasses—motorcycle glasses with reflective lenses. They had been expensive, real glass and all. He put them on, along with a spirit of arrogance, and backed the car out.

Pushing the stick shift hard into gear, Carlos burned rubber leaving the drive. As he drove, the madder he got. In this anger, he started muttering to himself in Spanish. Within the next few minutes, Carlos' unexplained feelings of hatred escalated to the threshold of violence. It was a good thing he didn't have a knife because right now he was ready to stab somebody. He looked in the rearview mirror as he pulled into a parking space at the church. The reflection of cold eyes in the motorcycle glasses looked back at him. I can escape from any prison. I go where I want, I do what I want, and nothing can stop me, he thought in Spanish.

"*Estoy listo para luchar!*" Carlos declared out loud, slamming the car door behind him.

Pastor Ken could see the arrogance in Carlos as they all came together in the small room for prayer. Carlos was speaking only Spanish, and though the others could not understand him, Pastor Ken, who also spoke Spanish, could. They sat together in a circle and began to worship God. Carlos, with his sunglasses still on, sat with arms folded, ankles crossed, wanting to kill somebody. Around him people prayed. One of the men came up to touch Carlos, but Pastor Ken grabbed his hand away. That's right, thought Carlos in Spanish. Touch me and I'll hit you. *No puedo esperar para luchar!* I can't wait to fight!

As these loving, caring people were readying to share his battle, unseen warriors were choosing up sides, angelic forces standing behind each saint. As the spiritual battle lines were drawn, Carlos' anger pulled him toward the enemy's side until he was face-to-face with . . . his *grandfather?* Instead of the weakness that he usually felt gazing into the blackness of Abuelo's eyes, now it was anger—anger for the abuse he had suffered at the hands of Abuelo. Without hesitation, he cursed Abuelo in Spanish.

"Are you ready to forgive your grandfather?" Pastor Ken asked.

Forgive Abuelo? Carlos wanted revenge. He wanted to punch him over and over again for the pain he caused. Angry Spanish curses spewed forth out of Carlos' mouth.

"I don't want to talk to you!" exclaimed Pastor Ken, "I want to talk to Carlos!"

Switching to English almost in mid-sentence, Carlos still had nothing but curses for Abuelo. The final soul battle had begun.

As the little group of prayer warriors prayed over Carlos, the heavenly angels stood shoulder to shoulder along the invisible path leading from God's throne to Carlos' heart. Soon when the power and the presence of God came upon Carlos, he took off his sunglasses, crushed them in his bare hands, and began to cry.

Falling to the floor, he let go of the glasses and wrestled with the hate he felt toward Abuelo, for burning him, for beating him, for trying to get rid of him.

"Father God, we pray that our brother Carlos here will choose to forgive his grandfather. We pray that you help him relinquish his desire to seek revenge and ask that you heal his damaged emotions," they prayed as they placed their hands on Carlos. Was it unforgiveness that was holding him in bondage to Satan? Yes, he could see that now. Though he had tried to submit everything to God, deep inside he had chosen to hold onto his anger and hatred for his grandfather. Carlos wrestled with himself until finally, lifting his hands to heaven, Carlos commanded Satan, in the name of Jesus Christ, to leave his mind and his presence . . . and in his heart of hearts, Carlos forgave Abuelo. The winged warriors rejoiced on their way home to heaven while the defeated demons slunk off to pursue other souls to enslave.

Satan had taken every advantage to justify and deceive Carlos into accepting that he didn't need to be healed from the hurts of his past. Yet it was through the spiritual conflict, that Carlos discovered what it meant to resist the devil, how to break free from spiritual bondage, and by whose power he would proclaim freedom to the captives of darkness. Because Jesus Christ had already crushed the enemy through his blood on the cross, Carlos could live fearless and free. His soul battle proved it, and now he was ready for the rest of his life.

"Uh, Carlos . . ." said Pastor Ken as he tapped him on the shoulder. Carlos turned from the others with whom he had been talking and rejoicing. "I have your sunglasses for you."

Pastor Ken poured a pile of shattered glass into Carlos' hands.

PART FOUR

Waynesboro, Pennsylvania

"A 19-year-old Waynesboro man was shot once in the chest outside a Security Road apartment complex early Sunday morning…"

—The Record Herald (March 15, 2004)

CHAPTER 26

If you confess with your mouth, "Jesus is Lord," and believe in your heart that God raised him from the dead, you will be saved.
(Romans 10:9)

On a Saturday night in March, police were summoned to an apartment complex in response to a loud disturbance. Two of the apartment's occupants had been threatened by three men, one of them with a handgun. This became the first incident that night.

Later in the evening, on his way to the same apartment, Jonathan knew that he was too far off the right path to even think about turning back. A few years ago, he'd made the effort to please his mother and at least go to the youth activities at the church. The girls had definitely been easy on the eyes, but the caring and the concern of the church people for him had made Jonathan feel uncomfortable.

So he'd held onto his style, wore his Jersey and baggy pants, his bandana and chains, and talked rap and smack throughout the music and the praying of the youth group. Yet, to his surprise, Jonathan had been touched by this God-thing the youth pastor talked about, and he'd begun to think that even he could be forgiven. He had thought it was real—that God's unconditional love for him was genuine. But he'd wished he hadn't known about it just yet, because then he'd had to make a choice. He'd had to decide what he would do about God loving his sorry self in spite of everything he'd done. In the end Jonathan had accepted the gift of eternal life.

Still, his natural loyalties had driven him back into the daily activities of his gang, and his social life had resumed as it had been before. Now he arrived at the apartment ready to mingle with the group already gathered there having a good time. This was his world, this was familiar. Jonathan was young (nineteen to be exact) and he was comfortable with life. Tonight was way too soon to be thinking about dying and too late to be worrying about how being in the wrong place and doing the wrong things would make it harder to find his way back to God.

At 12:40 A.M. Jonathan left the apartment with a few of his friends to head out to the parking lot—some to wait for rides, some to keep each other in the safety of their company. Their laughing and talking mingled with the night air when the three men returned again, emerging from the darkness. Taunts and threats were flaunted back and forth between the groups until finally one of the men opened fire.

The black asphalt rose up so fast that Jonathan never heard any of the five shots that were reported later by witnesses. He just knew that the left side of his chest radiated a pain so bad that he couldn't breathe. Lying in the darkness, he could feel the cold, hard gravel press through his clothes, chilling him to the bone. Squinting slightly he saw the tilted, swirling shoe tops and pant hems of his friends gathered around him. Dizzy, he closed his eyes again and listened to them yelling and screaming. Jonathan wanted to tell them that he was hurt, that it was too hard to breathe. Then, an odd stillness started to creep up his body from his toes, and soon the sound of commotion around him faded away until all he could hear was the soft, slowing thud of his heart.

According to the newspapers, the shooting was the second incident that had occurred at the residence. For Jonathan, it was the last.

The church people were saddened by Jonathan's death and stood by his mother in her grief and her planning of the funeral. Jonathan's killer was still at large and fearing an eruption of gang violence or a vendetta against Jonathan's younger brothers, the local high school was locked down during school hours. Finally on the appointed day, Jonathan's body was laid out in a casket and placed in the front of the church he had once tried to call his. The funeral director guided and arranged the events of the morning. The local police kept watch over Jonathan's many friends and acquaintances as they pulled into the church parking lot, dressed up, and smoking a final cigarette before finding a seat in the sanctuary. The youth were many and the church people few, but they were gathered together now to mourn for Jonathan.

Sight unseen, yet spiritually present, there were others occupying the minds and souls of some of the youth that entered the church as the funeral began. These beings tempered the hugs and the tears between Jonathan's friends creating illusions of true fellowship. The faithful Christians watched the whole process and thought the rituals and traditions demonstrated by Jonathan's friends were foreign and weird—the hand signs exchanged between the guys, the scraps of notes and the unconventional tokens left in the open casket, the accepted fashion, piercings, and tattoos that adorned their bodies. The church building itself was unfamiliar territory to the youth. They were convinced there was nothing for them within it. The kids were separate and different and had bought into their own culture believing that they belonged to the night, to each other, and that the here and now was the only thing worthy of their time and attention.

At 11 A.M. the youth pastor, who had been sitting in the front pew, stood and walked to the front of the church to start the service. Though dressed in a suit and tie, he carried himself as if he'd be more comfortable in jeans and a baseball cap. He was short, yet powerfully built like a boxer. His white hair accentuated his skin tone, which was dark like his father's. Though in his fifties, his energy and passion for living faith attracted the church teens. Jonathan, too, had thought the youth pastor understood him and cared about him. And because of that, Jonathan had believed in the loving God about whom the youth pastor had testified.

After opening prayer, the youth pastor sat down and Jonathan's brother Josh stood to speak. The crying had been muffled up to this point, but as Josh's voice became distorted by his tears, the sniffling among the youths in the audience grew in intensity. Finished with his tribute, Josh sat down, and the weeping and sobbing grew louder and more uncontrolled.

Then, unexpectedly, the church was filled with the throbbing bass beat of a rap song. High on the hit parade of hip hop, it had been requested and was now being played. The music spread like wave upon wave across the people there, and the teens that had been Jonathan's friends were captivated by it. Allowing for their grief to find expression in this way, the youth pastor sat quietly in the front pew praying.

It was unnoticeable at first, but one by one and then by twos and then by groups, teens started standing up all over the congregation. They gathered in the aisles of the church, hugging and crying out loud. They found each other, going to where one another sat, and embraced, sobbing. A few moved to the casket to cling and to mourn. Cries punctuated the din and an unnatural chaos began to take over the sanctuary. The music beat on carried by a vocal crescendo of souls possessed and destined for hell.

The surge of demonic presence felt all at once familiar to the youth pastor. The age-old enemy was still raging and preying upon the hearts of people. This time it had entered the church among the kids. The youth pastor looked up and immediately recognized the spirits of Azmaveth, Baanah, and Evi. Knowing he had the power to prevail against this enemy that he'd seen capture so many young adults, he got to his feet.

The youth pastor Carlos made his way through the clusters of Jonathan's friends around the sanctuary. The music and lyrics continued spreading wave after wave upon the people. Carlos looked at the funeral scene around him. "He has sent me to bind up the brokenhearted," Carlos recalled God's words. ". . . To proclaim freedom for the captives, and release from darkness for the prisoners." Carlos pushed past a group congregated around the casket and ascended the three steps in front. "To comfort all who mourn . . . and provide for those who grieve." Carlos gazed at the noise and confusion before him.

"Return to your seats," Carlos said. "Peace, be still. The battle is not against flesh," he silently addressed the disruptive spirits.

"Return to your seats," Carlos said a second time and the spirits heard. The raging music subsided.

"Return to your seats," Carlos voiced a third time, adding unspoken prayer—in Jesus' name. The spirits withdrew, expelled in one terrific gush out the back door of the sanctuary. The teens became calm and sat down.

Carlos looked out over the faces of the youth seated before him. He saw how they wore their lives, and he saw into their damaged souls that were so loved by God. Carlos bowed his head a moment before speaking, eyes resting on his hands clasped in front of him. These hands had plucked fruit in a tropical forest and fashioned sleds from banana leaves. They also had been burned by Abuelo's smoldering cigars. They had stolen goods, they had dealt drugs, and had bruised and beaten other human beings—shedding their blood, simply to prove his worth. Carlos had been a slave to whatever had mastered him in the past. But now his hands were as clean as his heart, having been washed in the blood of the righteous Son of God who loved him in spite of everything he had done. These hands were in chains no longer. With God as his witness, Carlos was desperate to offer his rescuer to the weak and wounded and lost that were on their way to death right in front of him. So he spoke to them and to all who would hear him.

"Do not let your heart be troubled. Trust in God. Trust also in me. In my Father's house are many rooms; if it were not so I would have told you. I am going there to prepare a place for you. And if I go and prepare a place for you, I will come back and take you to be with me that you also may be where I am.

"My story is not so unusual, my life not so amazing, for many of you have experienced being hurt by others, have known the desire to escape pain, have made the wrong choices, and have been prisoner to some of the desperate circumstances of life like I have. The Bible tells us that we all have sinned and that not one of us is perfect enough to be worthy to live in heaven with God when we die. In fact, the Bible also says that the sentence for being a sinner is death—death and hell.

"I was headed down that path . . . on my way to death. But the Bible also says that we are so loved by God that Jesus, the son of God, took on the death sentence for us. Jesus paid our penalty with His own life. And I am so glad, so grateful that I found that out in time. Whether you believe it or not, the case has been settled and we don't have to stay on death row. You are loved. God has been looking for you to tell you that since the day you were born. You have been loved since the beginning of all time, and God knows you and loves you no matter what.

"Are you hurting right now? Is someone you love just not there for you? Sometimes other people hurt us very badly either physically or mentally or even emotionally. Do you need to ease the pain?

"And how about the decisions you've had to make? Have the things you've done caused you or others harm? By giving in to pressure, have situations turned out to not be what you expected? Have you totally messed up on some really, really hard choices? And what about you? Do you feel lonely in a crowd, like no one cares about what happens to you, or that you can't trust anyone with your fears or your feelings?

"Just know that you are loved. Do not let your hearts be troubled about death or life or how much you've messed up. Trust in God—trust also in Me Jesus says. Trust Me with your life, for death is not the end; it is the doorway to eternity. Jesus says I go and prepare a place for you; I will come back and take you to be with Me that you also may be where I am.

"Now, it may happen when you are old, or maybe it could happen when you're young like Jonathan—when the door finally closes on this life. But here's the thing. When death comes, judgment happens. When death comes to you, your life in this world is over. Your life, with all of its choices, with all of the freedom to do whatever—all of it will be done. And then, judgment happens. That's the truth.

"When Jonathan got up the morning of his last day on earth, when he ate his breakfast, when he hung out with his friends, when he did whatever he did before going out that night, I'm sure he didn't expect to die. What about you? If it happens that your life is suddenly over today when you leave here, or tomorrow, or next week, or even a year from now—have you trusted Jesus enough so that you will be with Him in heaven forever?"

Carlos paused and he could feel the tears coming from deep within him. He listened to his own breathing and thought about the teens that sat before him. So many of them were going through what he had gone through, but now they needed to know what he knew—to find what he had found. Their idea of pleasure, their diminishing of sin's significance, and their seduction by the immoral and the unstable people in their lives weighed heavily on Carlos. How many had wandered off to follow in the way of his old adversary Balaam, who loved the wages of wickedness.

"Don't leave here without the gift. God is looking for you to give you the gift with your name on it. It is a free gift, one that I received and one that folks have been receiving for well over 2,000 years. It is the gift of new life, for both now and for your future—if only you will take it.

"We were created for eternal life with God. No matter what you've done, you are loved and you can be forgiven—the battle for your soul belongs to God."

EPILOGUE

Demonic spirits and satanic powers experienced by Carlos in this book are a reality, but encounters with the supernatural world here on earth only hint of the terror that hell really holds. We know that hell will mean separation from God, which is a condition no human being has yet experienced. Even now, God is with you, though you may think you're separated from God either by choice or by lifestyle. But the truth is that nothing can separate you from the love of God. Nothing you can do will make Him love you more than He already does, and there's nothing you can do that will make Him love you less.

God is as close to you as your breath. God so loved Carlos, Anna, Izzy, Efrain, and Hector—and *you*—that He sent His only Son to the earth. Believe in Him and death's doorway to eternity will not lead you to hell but to heaven's life everlasting. A door stands open in heaven for you and Jesus is the way. For God has loved you and has prepared a place for you since the beginning. Breathe. He is right beside you—and He's speaking your name.

Current Information on Carlos

Today, Carlos Rosado serves as Pastor of Outreach and Evangelism at Hollowell Brethren in Christ Church in Waynesboro, Pennsylvania. Carlos also works as a church planter, with the newest church, The Vine, starting in Smithsburg, Maryland. In addition, Carlos is on staff at Spring of Hope, a counseling ministry, where he continues to testify of the One who brings good news to the poor, binds up the brokenhearted, and proclaims freedom for those still prisoners to the spiritual darkness in their lives.

Carlos and Ruth, his wife of 33 years, raised four children, three of whom are still living and currently reside in Waynesboro, Pennsylvania.

Carlos can be contacted at soulbattlefortheheart@yahoo.com.

Spiritual Warfare Study/ Discussion Guide

"Finally, be strong in the Lord and in his mighty power. Put on the full armor of God so that you can take your stand against the devil's schemes. For our struggle is not against flesh and blood, but against the rulers, against the authorities, against the powers of this dark world and against the spiritual forces of evil in the heavenly realms."
Ephesians 6:10-12

The Reader's War Room

There are some wonderful study guides out there on spiritual warfare by knowledgeable authorities and dedicated ministers of the Gospel. They offer tons of in-depth information, scads of Bible verses, and untold inspirational insights. But this is not one of them.

This is simply the War Room behind the scenes of the book you've just read. You may enter the War Room discussion by yourself as one loved by God, or with those whom God has given *you* to love through Him (your small group or a fettered friend). In this War Room, imagine yourself standing with other warriors who have been given fullness in Christ, who is Head over every power and authority. We're here together, ready to share a few truths, reveal a few tactics, and set you up for success in spiritual skirmishes of your own.

And remember, as you get psyched to fight, God has taken everything that was against you and that stood opposed to you. He took it away, nailing it to the cross. He's already disarmed the powers of this world. See to it that no one takes you captive again through hollow and deceptive philosophy. Let no one deceive you by fine-sounding arguments. You are loved, you are His—and this means war!

Strategy One: Who is the Enemy?

Weapon: Revelation 12:7-9

The beginning of spiritual warfare is described in the introduction of Carlos's testimony. Balaam, Azmaveth, Baanah, and Evi are a few of the named demonic spirits. It is important to know the enemy.

- Refresh your memory about what these names mean, and then identify these or perhaps other spiritual enemies in your life.

- What are their names and how do you know them?

Strategy Two: What is the Enemy's Battle Plan?

Weapon: 2 Corinthians 4:3-4

Scripture tells us that the enemy's mission is to bind you and to blind you. The plan is to deceive the human race into living as prisoners to circumstance. Through lies and philosophies, Satan blinds people to what God has to offer—His love and salvation.

- What are some of the fears Satan used on Carlos to bind and to blind him?

- What does Satan use to bind or blind you?

- Specifically, how and when did the light of Christ first break through the enemy's plan for you? (Now is the time to work out your own personal testimony of how God rescued you!)

Strategy Three: Where are the Battlegrounds?

Weapon: Matthew 22:37-38

The enemy attacks through entry points or wounds of the heart, soul, and mind. Wherever the forces of darkness gain access, the battleground is established. The five battlefields are located in your mind, your will, your emotions, your body, and your relationships (shame, unfair criticism, rejection, divorce, rape, abuse, etc.).

- From the story, what are some of the ways Carlos fought demonic spirits in any of these five battlegrounds?

- On which battlefield is it toughest for you to fight the enemy?

- And through what wounds has Satan gained access?

Strategy Four: When Will the Enemy Attack?

Weapon: James 4: 7-10

The Bible tells us that the spirits of darkness attack when our resistance to Satan is low, when our hearts are not pure, and when we've moved away from God, neglecting to be humble or submit everything to Him. We can tell when this happens because sin will no longer seem wrong. Or, if we are convicted of sin, we might have very little motivation or lack the power to deal with it. Demonic spirits attack when they overtake these strongholds.

- What entrenched pattern of thought, value, or behavior that is contrary to biblical truth gave Satan a secure place of influence in Carlos' life?

- What have you accepted as an unchangeable part of life that perhaps allows Satan to consistently attack you? (Although, remember, as a Christian, your situation is NOT unchangeable!)

Strategy Five: How Do We Win and Stay Victorious?

Weapon: Ephesians 6:10-18

The people of God are called to wage war (2 Corinthians 10:3-5), but it is imperative that we remember that our authority in spiritual warfare flows out of our relationship with God (Zechariah 4:6). Winning strategy for every believer is simply found in the Bible.

- Exalt the Lord—read Philippians 2:9-11. How will you exalt the Lord in your own life?

- Read God's Word daily—read John 8:32. How will knowing His truth set you free?

- Stay in perfect relationship with God, repenting immediately of sin—read 1 John 1:9. What does God promise to do?

- Put on the whole armor of God—read again Ephesians 6:10-18. See following pages for prayer guidance in putting on the spiritual armor.

"I saw Satan fall like lightning from heaven. I have given you authority to trample on snakes and scorpions and to overcome all the power of the enemy; nothing will harm you. However, do not rejoice that spirits submit to you, but rejoice that your names are written in heaven" (Luke 10:18-20).

Exit the War Room, strong in the Lord, and mighty in His power . . .
C-H-A-R-G-E!

Prayer for Putting on the Spiritual Armor

Putting on the Belt

In the name of the Lord Jesus Christ, I claim the protection of the belt of truth, having buckled it securely around my waist. I pray the protection of the belt of truth over my personal life, my home and family, and the ministry God has appointed for my life. I use the belt of truth directly against Satan and his kingdom of darkness. I aggressively embrace Him who is the truth, the Lord Jesus Christ, as my strength and protection from all of Satan's deceptions. I desire that the truth of God's Word shall constantly gain a deeper place in my life. I pray that the truth of the Word of God may be my heart's delight to study and memorize.

Forgive me for my sins of not speaking the truth. Show me any way in which I am being deceived. By the Holy Spirit of truth, guide me into the practical understanding of words of truth. I ask the Holy Spirit to warn me before I deceive anyone and to ever protect me from believing Satan's lies. Thank you Lord, for making my local church a pillar and foundation for Your truth in my life. Help me to relate to my church and give protection and help to others as well as receive it myself.

I see, Lord Jesus Christ, that my ability to be invincibly strong and able to do Your will despite Satan's subtle ways requires the stabilizing power of the belt of truth. Thank you for providing this part of the armor. I take it gratefully and desire to have an ever-deepening understanding of its protection through Your power. Amen.

Claiming the Breastplate

In the name of the Lord Jesus Christ, I put on the breastplate of righteousness. In this moment, I repudiate any dependence I may have on my own goodness. I embrace the righteousness that is mine by faith in the Lord Jesus Christ. I look to the Holy Spirit to be effecting righteous actions, pure thoughts, and holy attitudes in my life. I hold up the righteous life of the Lord Jesus Christ to defeat Satan and his kingdom. I affirm that my victory is won and lived out by my Savior. I eagerly ask and expect that the Lord Jesus Christ shall live His righteousness through me. Through the precious blood of Christ, cleanse me of all my sins of omission and commission. Let me walk in a holy and clean manner that honors God and defeats the world, the flesh, and the devil, through Jesus Christ my Lord. Amen.

Appropriating Peace

Loving heavenly Father, by faith and in the name of the Lord Jesus Christ, I put on the shoes of peace. I accept Your declaration that I am justified and that I have peace with You. May my mind grasp the wondrous truth with everincreasing awareness. I thank You Lord, that I need not carry any anxiety or suffer from inner torment of turmoil. Thank You, Lord Jesus Christ, that You have invited me to make all of my needs known to You through prayer. Teach me to walk in Your presences until the inner peace of God, which transcends human understanding, replaces my anxiety. I desire to know the strong presence of Your peace. May You walk with me and say to me, "Don't be afraid: I will help you."

With all of my heart I want to be obedient to Your will at all times. May the fullness of Christ who is my peace enable me to so walk in Him that the fullness of His peace may glorify God through me. I take the shoes of peace in the name of the Lord Jesus Christ and by faith shall walk in them this day. Amen.

Taking Up the Shield

Loving heavenly Father, I take by faith the protection of the shield of faith. I count upon Your holy presence to surround me like a capsule, offering total protection from all of Satan's flaming arrows. Grant me the grace to accept Your refining purpose in allowing any of Satan's arrows to pass through the shield and even to praise You for it. Help me to concentrate upon Your presence and not the enemy's arrows.

In the name of the Lord Jesus Christ I claim the protection of the holy angels to guard and shield me from the assaults of Satan's kingdom. May these ministering angels be present to interfere with the strategy of Satan to harm me and my family. I appropriate the victory of the blood of the Lord Jesus Christ and hold it against the advances of the evil one. With gratitude and praise, in the name of the Lord Jesus Christ I rejoice in Your victory. Amen.

Putting on the Helmet

Loving heavenly Father, I take by faith the helmet of salvation. I recognize that my salvation is the Person of Your Son, the Lord Jesus Christ. I cover my mind with Him. I desire that He put His mind within me. Let my thoughts be His thoughts. I open my mind fully and only to the control of the Lord Jesus Christ. Replace my own selfish and sinful thoughts with His. I reject every projected thought of Satan and his demons and request instead the mind of the Lord Jesus Christ. Grant to me the wisdom to discern thoughts that are from the world, my old sin nature, and Satan's kingdom.

I praise you, heavenly Father, that I may know the mind of Christ as I hide Your Word within my heart and mind. Open my heart to love Your Word. Grant to me the facility and capacity to memorize large portions of it. May Your Word be ever over my mind like a helmet of strength, which Satan's projected thoughts cannot penetrate. Forgive me for my neglect, my failure to aggressively take the salvation always available to me. Help me to fulfill the discipline of daily duty to appropriate Your salvation. These things I lay before You in the precious name of my Savior, the Lord Jesus Christ. Amen.

Taking up the Sword

In the name of the Lord Jesus Christ, I lay hold of the sword of the Spirit, the Word of God. I embrace its inerrant message of truth and power. I humbly ask the Holy Spirit to guide me into true understanding of the message of the Word. Grant to me the discipline and dedication to memorize the Word and to saturate my mind with its truth and power.

In the name of the Lord Jesus Christ and by the ministry of the Holy Spirit, grant to me the wisdom to always apply the Word against the enemy. May I use the Word to defeat Satan and to advance the cause of Christ into that very realm Satan claims. Amen.

Taken from *Overcoming the Adversary* by Mark I. Bubeck

Carlos' Glossary of Spiritual Warfare Terminology

- **Ancestral Sins**—sins, weakness, proneness to certain sins that are passed down in families from generation to generation. These are passed on behaviorally, by observation and by actual internal learning. Examples would be alcoholism, fornication and pre-marital conception, gossip or slander, and a critical spirit.

- **Besetting Sins**—sins, weaknesses, fleshly desires that are acted upon over and over even though, as a believer, he/she may not want to do so. They are usually the ones you find yourself repenting of the most.

- **Curses**—are vows or non Christian "prayers" said over a family or individuals. These have profound impact on the life of a child. A curse could be "You are so stupid, you're worthless." A curse could be Masonic ritual "prayers" or having had pow-wow witchcraft practitioners in one's family. Curses are lived out when taken into an individual's heart.

- **Demon Possession**—is the actual inhabiting of a human being by one or more evil spirits that actually control the person beyond their will. Demon-possessed people are driven to act out evil even though they may not want to.

- **Demonization**—to be drawn to certain patterns of behavior that a believer can't seem to shake. For example, a person who is demonized by a spirit of lust just can't seem to shake the leaning toward pornography or lustful movies.

- **Entry Points/Wounding**—wounds of the heart are very often entry points for the forces of darkness to establish new footholds or even strongholds in the life of a believer. Wounds can be shame, unfair criticism, rejection, divorce, rape, abuse, and so on.

- **Footholds**—an area in a believer's life the enemy holds and is seeking to erect a work upon. A foothold could be an offense a person has chosen not to forgive.

- **Soul Ties**—ancestral sin issues, besetting sin issues, curses, wounds, true/false belief systems that pass between mates through sexual intercourse. Becoming one flesh is to establish soul ties to the person. Other examples include: blood brothers, cult members, strong friendship, and business relationship bonds.

- **Strongholds**—an entrenched pattern of thought, value, or behavior that is contrary to Biblical truth and gives the Devil a secure place of influence in a person's life.

- **True/False Belief Systems**—things we believe about ourselves or life in general that can be true or totally false. For instance, a person may believe God is angry at them or that God loves them and is gracious to them. It's important to have the child in the person believe this and not just the adult (emotion and intellect).

- **Unforgiveness**—a tremendously powerful spiritual issue of the human heart. To embrace this spirit is to doom health and wholeness within. To nurse a grudge in the heart is to invite a bitter spirit, demonization, or even ultimately possession. It also prevents one from receiving a blessing.